THE
HOUSE HUNTER'S
HANDBOOK

Joan Zunde is a qualified architect and, after practising in Coventry and Birmingham, is now Senior Lecturer in Construction Technology at Sheffield City Polytechnic. She has written two previous books, *Design Procedures* and *Design Technology*, as well as a series of 24 articles entitled *Know Your House*. She lives in Sheffield with her husband Peter, who is also an architect and who provided the drawings for this book, and their two daughters.

THE HOUSE HUNTER'S HANDBOOK

a step-by-step guide to finding and
buying a home

Joan Zunde

illustrated by Peter Zunde

MACMILLAN LONDON

First published 1983 by
PAPERMAC
a division of Macmillan Publishers Limited
4 Little Essex Street London WC2R 3LF
and Basingstoke

Associated companies in Auckland, Dallas, Delhi, Dublin,
Hong Kong, Johannesburg, Lagos, Manzini, Melbourne,
Nairobi, New York, Singapore, Tokyo, Washington and Zaria

ISBN 0 333 33127 3 (hardcover)
ISBN 0 333 33128 1 (Papermac)

Printed in Hong Kong

Contents

Chapter 9 **Alterations and extensions**

Chapter 10 **The decision to go ahead**

Chapter 11 **The actual purchase**

Chapter 12 **The financial maze**

Acknowledgements

I would like to thank the many people who have contributed to my experience and understanding of the upheaval of finding a new home. These include my parents, in whose company I obtained a thorough elementary grounding in the subject, as well as the friends and family with whom I have househunted over the years.

In all I have had twelve homes, ranging in age from 300 years to brand new, and in size from one-and-a-half rooms up. They have included converted and purpose-built flats and terraced, semidetached and detached houses.

I must warmly acknowledge the friendly and supporting guidance of Julia Vellacott as editor, and the help of many people at the publishers who have performed miracles of decipherment and organisation.

Finally I must thank my daughters Ingrid and Helga for endless patience and cups of coffee, and my husband Peter for his encouragement and meticulous drawings.

Joan Zunde
Sheffield
1982

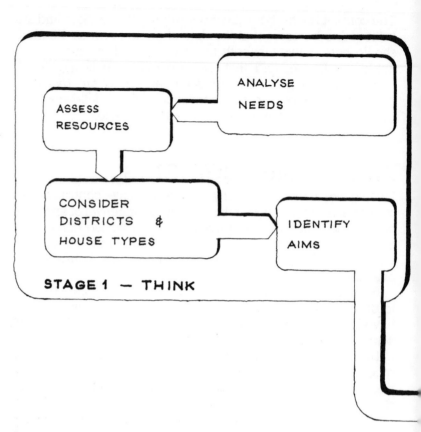

ANALYSE NEEDS

ASSESS RESOURCES

CONSIDER DISTRICTS & HOUSE TYPES

IDENTIFY AIMS

STAGE 1 — THINK

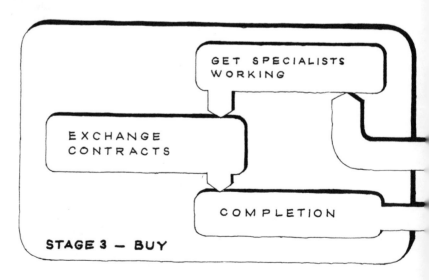

GET SPECIALISTS WORKING

EXCHANGE CONTRACTS

COMPLETION

STAGE 3 — BUY

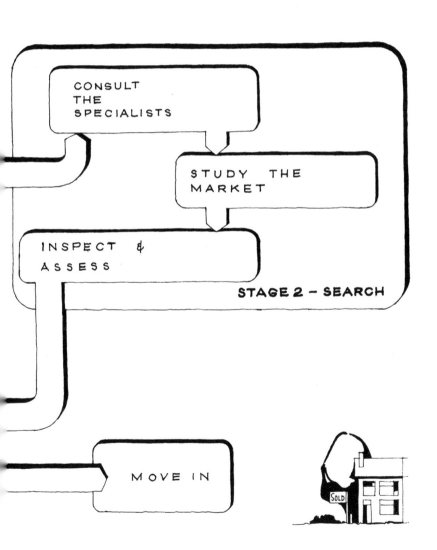

CONSULT
THE
SPECIALISTS

STUDY THE
MARKET

INSPECT &
ASSESS

STAGE 2 – SEARCH

MOVE IN

SOLD

Your needs – and some notes on housing standards

Your needs

Your particular family is unique, and it needs an equally individual home. We can be told what an 'average' household is like, how it spends its time and how much space it needs, but few if any households actually fit that 'average' mould. They range from single people investing their earnings and getting 'into' the housing market to elderly couples needing compact, easily run places to retire in; from large families of active kids to unrelated groups sharing a purchase.

The essential first step in finding a home which suits *your* needs is to take a cool look at what those needs are. I can't possibly do this for you, but I can suggest a number of questions you should consider, so as to work them out for yourselves. That is the purpose of this chapter.

I have also included some notes on what are generally thought to be the points to look for in some specific areas. These give standards that apply to most households – but never forget that you are not 'most households', but *unique*. (Subjects discussed in the first half of the chapter include a cross reference to the second half.)

Bear in mind that we are all predisposed in favour of an arrangement we're used to. It's valuable to make an effort to escape from this and imagine what other set-ups would actually be like, because our present accommodation may be forcing us into patterns of activity that we wouldn't naturally adopt. First-time buyers need to be especially rigorous in working out their needs, as this is probably the first time they've had a chance to control their own surroundings. On the other hand, there is one group, those to whom the purchase is first and foremost an investment, who should choose the safest and most conventional home, which is easiest to sell, irrespective of their life style. In most parts of the country this would be a two–three-bedroom estate house, though in London it might be an older property.

Family

How many of you are there?

Do you expect to increase the family? Might grandparents join you? Are teenagers likely to become students, join the forces or set up on their own? Bear in mind that you may be in the same place for ten or twenty years, that you won't want moves forced upon you, and try to take into account the changes that time will bring.

How old are you all?

If you are setting up home with a view to establishing a family, you will have to consider the needs of small children quite carefully (as well as the new life style they bring their parents). Imagine the plight of a parent living in a fourth-floor flat with no lift or garden, bringing home two toddlers and the shopping, and compare this with the situation of the same household in a neat two-storey home with an enclosed garden that can be reached direct from the living room.

Similarly, you may need to exercise your imagination if you are choosing a retirement home. However active you are at present, you need to consider that stairs may be at best an obstacle and at worst a hazard in a few years' time, and that compact, easily cared-for space is really what you will require.

Ask yourself whether anyone is at special risk because they're very young or very old. Consider safety carefully if you're elderly.

Good lighting on stairs, cupboards you can reach without stretching and handles by baths and toilets may not seem vital at present but may make the difference between staying in your own home and having to move to sheltered accommodation in ten years' time

How are you related (if at all)?

How much privacy do you want, and what are the special feelings of your household about this? Do you care who hears your conversations or watches you bath, or not?

Are any of you disabled, and if so how does that affect the home? What pets do you have?

Bedrooms

It's generally considered that a single room should have a minimum of 7 sq m (77 sq ft), and a double room a minimum area of 11 sq m (121 sq ft) (though we have all seen ingenious arrangements in caravans which use much less space than that). If a room is to serve a second purpose (sewing, study) extra space or very carefully devised furniture will be needed. See p. 9 for more details.

Who needs a room to him/herself?

Do you need a spare room for visitor(s) or space in some other room?

Should any of the bedrooms have space for hobbies, study, play or sitting?

Do you want built-in wardrobes? Note that these make good use of space – so long as you haven't got wardrobes already.

Bathrooms, toilets and washing arrangements

Your requirements will be very much influenced by your modesty, the length of time you linger in the bath and the size of the family. A bathroom, separate WC, groundfloor cloakroom and bedroom basins may be considered perfect, but consider alternatives such as the possibility of a shower in the bedroom, or basin in the loo and so on. See p. 10.

Do you need basins in bedrooms?

How many baths do you need? Where should they be? Must there be a bath on every floor that has bedrooms? Should any be en suite with bedrooms? Do you need a tub at all? 3

How many WCs do you need? Where should they be? If you have a groundfloor loo in mind, should it be near the front door or easily accessible from the garden?

Do you want a bidet? If so, where?

How many showers do you need? Where should they be?

Could you use a bathroom for laundry? A laundry/cloakroom near to the kitchen can be a convenient arrangement for a family often in the garden or with children. If there is anyone disabled who sleeps downstairs, it could also contain a shower.

All this sounds pretty palatial, but it's simply a group of suggestions of less conventional arrangement you might like or hate but need to be prepared for.

Stairs

Are there any rooms which *must* be on the top floor? For example, a studio, or a bedroom for someone nervous.

Are there any rooms which *must* be on the ground floor? Possibly all of them for the disabled or elderly. Note that the Regency arrangement that puts the main living space on the first floor lifts that room above the traffic, and often allows a view to be exploited.

Do you want to limit the number of staircases, and therefore the number of floors? A house with attic and cellar has three flights, all of which have to be maintained and heated. And climbed. See p. 12.

Living spaces

What do you *do* in your living room?
This is a key question, and deserves detailed thought. It's a good idea, and revealing, to keep a detailed diary setting out the amount of time spent entertaining, watching TV, listening to records, playing scrabble or whatever. This may give you a clearer idea of the amount of space you need. Groups of friends sharing may discover they don't actually need a 'living room' at all – good sized individual bed-sitting rooms would be more convenient, though they're bound to want some neutral, shared space.

How often, and how formally, do you entertain?

Where do you prefer to eat formal and informal meals? Surveys indicate that everyone wants to eat in the kitchen sometimes and often on their knees before the TV, but are you 'everyone'?

How often does the family sit down together to a formal meal? You may discover that you don't need a dining room at all, and could use the space better for another purpose.

4

If you do need a dining room, can it have a secondary use? Dining rooms double conveniently as studies, TV rooms or music rooms, but not as spare bedrooms.

Do you need a study? If you intend to run a business from home or mark homework, you will need somewhere to keep your papers and work undisturbed.

Do you need a music room? If you play the trombone in the works band or are a rock addict, you need a room where you'll neither disturb nor be disturbed by other people.

Either a study or a music room can double as a guest room.

Do you need a playroom? This might be for small children, in which case it needs to be near at hand, or for older people who want to leave a train layout or computer set up.

How much connection do you want between living spaces indoors and out? Is the outdoors space for meals, for play or just for a pleasant outlook? See p. 6 and also under 'Garden', p. 127.

Kitchen

How much cooking do you *really* do?

What other activities do you want to carry on in the kitchen? Kitchens are probably used for more varied purposes than any other part of the house, yet we all tend to accept the conventional view of a 'dream' kitchen that may not suit our life style at all. Again, a diary might be revealing.

How many stores do you keep?

What appliances do you own?

Do you want to eat in the kitchen? If so, how many of you at once, and how often? Does everybody eat at once?

Do any pets live in the kitchen? Unhygienic, but very common! See p. 14.

Utility room

Is this intended for laundry, storage, dirty hobbies, pets, other uses?

Should it be self-contained, or can it be a part of the kitchen or a passageway into the garden?

What services does it need? See p. 16.

Hobbies

Are your hobbies clean or dirty? That is to say, are they socially acceptable in living rooms (embroidery, philately) or do they need to be segregated? Music practice, pottery or motor-cycle maintenance might come into the second category.

How much space do they need?

How much storage is required?

Do they need electricity, water, drainage, good lighting, a washable floor?

Storage

Consider what you *need* or specially want to have room for, and put your possessions under headings to work out how much room they need and where it should be. It's best to keep things nearest to where they'll be used, and to have the most regularly used things in the most accessible places. Headings might include:

- cool storage, e.g. photographic equipment, dry stores,
- warm conditions, e.g. linen, clothes,
- dry conditions, e.g. sports gear, cassettes,
- well-ventilated conditions, e.g. books, vegetables.

Some things may appear on more than one list.

Make sure that you have taken all the following into account: food, utensils, outdoor clothes, out-of-season clothes, games kit, linen, unused furniture and curtains, musical instruments, records, books, suitcases, photographs, films, video cassettes, bicycles, garden tools, ladder, fuel, cot, baby bath and pram (between babies), wheelchair, mementoes.

Garage

Calculations have been published suggesting that providing your car with a garage isn't cost-effective. However, garages are used for many other purposes. See p. 18.

What is the biggest car to which you're likely to aspire?

Can the garage serve as workshop, storage space, play space?

Must it be reached under cover?

Might there be more than one car?

Granny flat

Do you need space for a self-contained flat under the same roof?

Is this for someone elderly, or for an au pair, to rent out, or to use as an office/consulting room?

Garden

Is this to be an extension of living space, provide a buffer from the world, give safe play space, grow vegetables, grow flowers, dry laundry, give parties?

Do you need a tool shed?

Do you need a greenhouse?

Do you want access to the garden that's not through the house?

If you're looking for a flat, do you want a private garden, a shared garden, no garden at all?
See p. 52.

Heating

Do you prefer one particular fuel? It can be expensive to change if the 'wrong' one is installed.

Do you want automatic time and temperature controls?

In a flat, do you want heat provided as part of the service, or do you want independent heating?
See p. 18.

District

Are you town, suburb or country people? Living in a town gives you good access to services and facilities at the price of constant bustle. It cuts costs and time spent on travelling to live near to work, but rates may be high.

Suburban life often means a modern home, and modern schools and shops. In spite of snide comment, it provides precisely what most people want, because it is designed to.

The country is peaceful and may be cheaper, but transport and other services may be difficult.

If you're trading up-market, consider the alternatives of getting a similar home to your present one but in a 'posher' district, or getting a better house in the same district.

Are you retiring to your new home? If so, consider carefully before moving away from family and friends. You are likely to become less mobile as the years progress, and to be increasingly dependent on having someone who can pop in regularly. Some of the popular retirement areas, such as the south coast, have very big concentrations of the elderly in their populations and very strained social services.

Chapter 5 gives detailed material on districts: see p. 93.

Summing up your needs

Once everyone concerned has had their say, and the answers to each of these questions which is relevant to your case has

been beaten out (as well as other points which are important to you but which I haven't foreseen), you are in a position to describe your ideal home.

I suggest you try to avoid specifying the number of rooms, or the age of the building, or precisely where it's going to be, and concentrate on the activities and possessions the flat, cottage or house has to accommodate.

Be very clear that it's unlikely that the *perfect* answer to your dreams exists. You must be clear which of the items in your list are essential, which are desirable, and which are merely frills that would be nice if they came along. You need to know where you are prepared to compromise and where you have to dig your heels in.

Having thought so exhaustively about what you are looking for, you should find that you are spared endless visits to properties that are in fact quite unsuitable – but you may at times feel that there simply doesn't exist a place that is remotely suitable that you can afford. Don't despair. Go on searching. You are bound, if you are realistic, to find the right house in the right place at the right price in the end.

It may be wise, having reached this point, to measure your present home against your list of requirements. If you are not obliged to move to take up a new job, you might find that spending the cost of a move on improving your present home is the most cost-effective way of getting what you want. Read Chapter 9 on Alterations and Extensions.

Notes on standards in housing

Up to this point I have suggested that you should consider your own personal and particular needs. The rest of the chapter summarises some commonly accepted standards of good accommodation. Your needs may be better met by some other arrangement, but it's helpful to know what is usually considered desirable.

Bedrooms

The drawings show the sizes of the major groups of furniture that are usually put into bedrooms, study bedrooms and bedsitting rooms.

Beds should not be put under windows, and if they have to be arranged along walls, bedmaking can be difficult.

One light, whether it is a ceiling one or a table lamp, should be switchable from the bed. The Department of the Environment suggests that there should be three socket outlets in the master bedroom and two in each other one: some would think this too few. A dressing table needs good natural light, and this

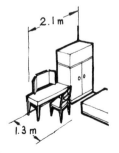

9

2.9 m

2.55 m

probably means putting it at right angles to the window rather than under it.

It is often convenient for a bedroom to be planned with a recess that a wardrobe can go into (it seems less bulky there) or to which doors can be fixed to make a built-in wardrobe. The depth behind the doors needs to be at least 0·5 m (1 ft 8 in).

Traditionally, bedroom doors open so as to shield the view of the room. Not everyone finds this convenient, however – but it's difficult to change the arrangement you find, because of the light switch, so you're usually stuck with it.

A door in a corner sterilises space on two walls, and one at least 300 mm (12 in) from a corner is better.

If you put furniture in front of a radiator, you lose a lot of heat and may damage the furniture.

Bathroom

The Department of the Environment Design Bulletin 'Spaces in the Home – Bathrooms and WCs' is an invaluable reference.
Position Houses should be designed to provide economical service layouts, and it's therefore better (other things being equal) to have the bathroom sited above the kitchen than to have it in some remote corner of the building. Similarly, in flats, bathrooms are planned close to kitchens, and the bathrooms and kitchens of all the flats are arranged above one another. Cloakrooms and basins in bedrooms should also be close to the service runs. Other arrangements can produce trouble of two

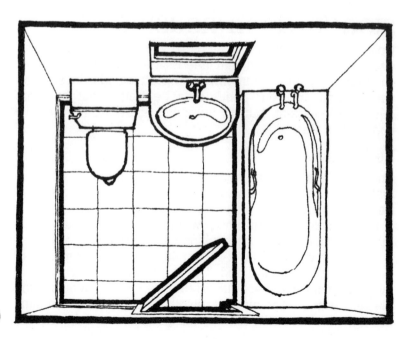

kinds: the length of hot-water pipes causes waste and long waits for hot water, and long waste pipes can result in poor outflow.

The position of a bathroom or cloakroom doesn't matter quite so much as the convenient siting of the kitchen, excepting that some households may find it important to have a downstairs cloakroom near either the front or rear entrance.

Space There should be room not only for the fittings required but also for the users, and sometimes this means an adult bathing two children. The drawing gives some guidelines. In general, it is difficult to arrange a convenient bathroom with WC in a space less than 2 m × 1·8 m (6 ft 8 in × 6 ft), and one where the WC is elsewhere in less than 1·5 m × 1·8 m (5 ft × 6 ft). A WC on its own needs 1·8 m × 0·9 m (6 ft × 3 ft). If there is a bidet or shower, additional space is usually essential, though a shower over the bath will do. Showers should have mixer valves and be of the handheld type if they are to suit all the family.

There should be somewhere to hang clothes, towels and possibly wet washing as well, and usually a store for dirty linen. A bathroom is sometimes thought a suitable place for a washing machine.

Heating Safe heating at all times of year is needed. A wall-fixed electric radiator with pull switch is often the most suitable fitting. Heat from a hot water cylinder shouldn't be relied on: the cylinder should be too well lagged for this to be effective, and in any case ought really to be sited outside the bathroom, because if (as is usually the case) the cupboard is used for linen, this will tend to get damp from a bathroom atmosphere.

Lavatory High-level flushing cisterns are obsolescent, and suites where the cistern is coupled directly to the closet without a flush pipe are best.

Bath A sunken bath is not always easier to climb in and out of, and the headroom it takes up on the floor below can be a nuisance. Handgrips on both sides of baths, on the other hand, are helpful to almost everyone.

Materials of fittings There is a wide range of materials used for fittings, most of them perfectly sound, but look out for enamel on cast iron, in older baths, which stains and chips and may even wear thin. Glass-reinforced plastic or acrylic baths are slightly flexible, so the joint between the bath and the wall is hard to waterproof. The commonest material in modern homes is vitreous china.

Other finishes All finishes on walls and floors, including carpeting, should be washable and warm.

Boxroom

Quite often one finds a house described as 'four-bedroomed' when it has one room barely big enough to take a bed, let alone 11 anything else. A glory hole for dumping can in fact be invaluable, and provide a perch for an occasional guest. It can also, if imaginatively fitted out, provide the workroom or hobbies room which is a virtual necessity to many.

To count as a habitable room, it needs a window and proper headroom of at least 2·30 m (7 ft 8 in).

Landing

Space on the landing is almost entirely wasted space, but has to be decorated, heated and carpeted. The smaller it is, the better – providing, of course, that you can get in and out of the rooms and can maneouvre some pretty bulky furniture. It is dangerous to have any room door right at the head of the stairs: 300 mm (1 ft) is the minimum distance, though 900 mm (3 ft) is better. This is about the width of a door.

Stairs

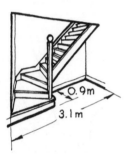

Stairs with straight flights are the safest and most economical – and usually the easiest to get furniture up and down, though a dog-leg stair with a decent well is good for this too. There should be enough head room for you not to feel you need to duck, and in a small house this often means there is a raised bulkhead in one of the bedrooms (sometimes with a built-in wardrobe on it). Straight stairs are the easiest to carpet, and the carpet can be moved from time to time to even out wear.

If there are 'winders' – wedge-shaped treads – there shouldn't be more than three to get round a right angle or they would be too narrow to step on safely, and they should be at the bottom of a flight, never at the top (because they are bound to be a hazard, and missing your step at the top of the stairs is a lot worse than doing so at the bottom). There shouldn't – for similar safety reasons – be sets of less than three treads, or, particularly, single steps down to quarter landings.

A handrail on at least one side should give a firm grip at a convenient height. It is a matter of preference whether there are ballusters under this or the space is panelled (if it's on the hall side), but there shouldn't be a gap anyone could fall through.

Good daylight and artificial light are very important on stairs.

In blocks of flats, stairs are important as fire escapes. They should be entirely built and finished with materials that won't burn easily, and should lead you down directly to the open air. At the landings, they should be closed off with doors which are kept closed, to stop smoke from spreading. There ought to be an alternative escape route, preferably down a second stair.

Dining space

The space set aside for meals, whether it's a separate room or part of the living room or kitchen, must be big enough to accommodate the table at its full extension, people sitting round it, and someone passing behind the chairs to change the plates – but not much else. If there's a sideboard to go in, space to get to it while the table's in use could be needed.

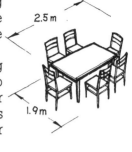

It's generally better to have a dining room that's only just big enough, and extra space in the general living area, than two living rooms of roughly equal size as is often found, for constructional reasons, in older houses. 3 m (10 ft) square is often big enough, especially if the space is a wing of another room.

There should be at least two thirteen-amp socket outlets.

The dining space should be near the kitchen, or it tends not to get used. Service hatches are controversial: probably the best kind is long and low, so that everything can be lined up from one side and picked up from the other by the same person when they've gone round. Small ones need two people to work effectively. Hatches let smells into dining rooms.

Living space

The Department of the Environment, whose Design Bulletin 'Space in the Home' is very informative and useful, envisage that a family will have an easy chair for each person (two might be in the form of a couch), a TV and some tables, and not much else except sewing box, toy box, bookcase, record player, and this is what a modern home is designed to accommodate in the living area.

There should be five well-distributed socket outlets.

Good daylight and a pleasant view are important. A sunny aspect may not be quite so vital. Although many people love a sunny room, some draw curtains against the danger of faded carpets, and many would enjoy sitting in the shade looking out at a sunny garden as much as having the sun in their eyes.

Too big a living room is actually a disadvantage, because the size of a 'conversation group' is limited.

Open plan

There are various degrees of open planning, from the simple dining-kitchen up to elaborate split-level arrangements. Whatever the space, this is usually most 'liveable' if the room is arranged so that different areas for different purposes are clearly defined, even though they may flow into one another.

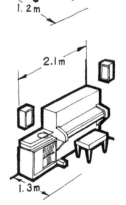

There is usually a lack of wall space to stand furniture against, so that the backs of sideboards and bookcases have to be on view.

The space should be well insulated from outdoors, and there *must* be a porch if the front hall has been thrown into the living room or an open-planned kitchen leads directly to outside.

If stairs rise from an open-planned area, the house can be expensive to heat, because heat rises, and the bedrooms are 13 warmed before the living area. If, on the other hand, the open-planned living area is on the upper floor with bedrooms and ancillary spaces below, this problem doesn't arise.

Unless a family is hooked on the smell of baking bread, and can guarantee never to burn the custard, it is essential to have an extractor fan in the kitchen of an open-plan house.

Conservatory/sunlounge

There are various types of extensions to houses which are claimed to increase their usefulness. Most of these should be looked at with some scepticism – many are so narrow that they do little but provide a place to keep garden chairs and toys, which may be useful, but is it worth the sacrifice of a view of the garden and natural lighting? Many, too, have a great deal of glass which may leak heat at an alarming rate, but which is also prohibitively expensive to double-glaze.

Another snag, especially with traditional conservatories in, for example, Victorian houses, can be that the glass roof isn't protected. In a really bad winter snow off the roof can descend in an avalanche and smash it. Although household insurance may cover this, the damage is none the less upsetting and dangerous and there should be snowboards along the gutter above to stop it from happening.

Kitchen

The Department of the Environment Design Bulletin 'Spaces in the Home – Kitchens and Laundering Spaces' is a useful

reference book. Your local library should have it or will get it for you.

A kitchen is a workspace, and like any other should be arranged so that it can be efficient and safe. Size is in the long run less important than arrangement, and very convenient arrangements can be made within very small spaces. In general, a working kitchen should have a total floor area of at least 9 sq m (100 sq ft), with extra space for meals if they are to be eaten there.

Doors in the corner of the room sterilise wall space on two walls, and make it difficult to arrange fittings so as to exploit the available space to the full. Ideally there should be only *one* door, at least 0·5 m (1 ft 8 in) from a corner.

The best arrangement for *working surfaces* in a kitchen is as follows: worktop/sink/ worktop/hob/worktop. One of the work-tops near the sink may be a drainer. The sequence shouldn't be interrupted by a door or a passageway, but may be arranged around a corner or in a U-shape. The more worktop provided the better.

Windows There is no magic in placing a sink under a window, as is so often done: this happens to be easy from the point of view of drainage, but is at the expense of other convenience. You would be better served by a sink at right angles to the window wall, and a window which is entirely accessible for cleaning – and to sit by over a meal. If the cooker is near to a window, special precautions are needed to protect it from draughts, and *no curtains* must be hung.

Table heights A suitable height for rolling out pastry is one on which you can rest your knuckles while standing without stooping or bending your arms. You should be able to do this in the base of a sink. For chopping or ironing a higher level is more suitable, while to beat eggs a lower surface is more comfortable. Add to this variety the fact that not only the housewife but her 5 ft grandmother, her infant daughter and her 6 ft 4 in husband may all want to cook, and you will see why adjustable table heights are often advocated!

The usual worktop height today is around 900 mm (3 ft), but this is only a compromise, and best augmented by a table at 750 mm (2 ft 6 in).

Storage As we saw in the first part of this chapter, it is important to have three types of storage: dry goods, in a cool dry cupboard; perishables, in the fridge and freezer (best out of the kitchen, as it quickly frosts up there); china and utensils.

As far as possible, each article should be stored near to where it will be used, and items in regular use should be most accessibly stored. Suitable cupboard heights are shown in the drawing. On the whole, special interior fittings are more limiting than helpful: straightforward shelving and drawers are more flexible in use.

15

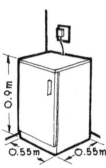

Appliances Wherever possible, it is helpful to have appliances built into a run of fittings, making cleaning easy. Avoid if at all possible arrangements with washing-up machines and so on on top of worktops: the worktop is too valuable to use in that way. All such machines and cookers make demands on the services, but the appliance should be conveniently placed and the service brought to it, never the appliance placed where the service happens to be handy. The service requirements and typical sizes of common appliances are shown in the drawing.

Open planning Provided there is good artificial air extraction from the cooking area, open planning of kitchen and living areas has many attractions, except to those people who prefer to keep the inevitable mess of cooking out of sight. The cook is not cut off from the rest of the household, and can talk to friends or supervise children's play, and there is an added feeling of space.

Utility room A utility room is often, but not invariably, thought of mainly as a laundry: it may also be used for storage and hobbies. Its relationship to the kitchen, the rest of the house and the garden needs to be considered in the light of the purposes for which a particular household will use it. A width of 1·5 m (5 ft) is barely enough to work in.

Services Good lighting in kitchens and utility areas is essential, and should include lights over working surfaces as well as good general lighting.

There should be enough power points above worktop level for all the appliances which might be needed at one time (mixer, blender, toaster, slicer, iron, clock, heating boiler, kettle). Parker Morris, in the very important postwar report on the design of homes, *Homes for Today and Tomorrow*, which came out in 1961, recommended a minimum of four sockets in a working kitchen, and the number of appliances and gadgets in use has proliferated since then. I would suggest six might be adequate, provided they are conveniently distributed. The cooker needs to be permanently wired to a separate thirty-amp circuit. *None* of the points should be near to a sink.

Hot and cold water must be available at at least one sink, and possibly at more than one. They may also be needed as permanent supplies to washing machines and washing-up machines. A bucket tap is useful.

A gas supply may be provided to a cooker, a boiler and to a space heater. There should be flues to all heating appliances, and this may oblige you to put them in a particular place.

Air extraction is good. It both removes cooking smells and minimises condensation. There could be a fan either in a window or built into a wall: in either case it should be as close to the cooker as possible. Some fans are driven electrically and some work by differential air pressure (and are rather less effective).

16

Most kitchens need some source of heat besides the cooker, and the heating boiler isn't the best way of providing this, as it should be efficiently lagged. An 'instant' radiator, gas or electric, is most convenient as it can be switched off when the room heats up.

See also the section on services which begins on p. 18.

Finishes The finishes to floors, walls and ceilings, cupboards and worktops should all be fixed with as few joints as possible, and be hardwearing. Worktops come in a wide range of materials, of which teak is possibly the best but melamine the commonest. The latter doesn't stand up well to chopping. A material which neither damages knives nor is damaged by them is best for this purpose, while a cool one (stainless steel is used in commercial kitchens) is best for pastry making. Tile, proving the joints are neat, is a good all-round compromise.

A floor finish which is easy to clean, which is warm and reasonably resilient to walk on, and which resists spills of grease and water is essential. Ceramic tiles are probably ideal, but where the floor is a suspended one these are impractical, and vinyl tiles are a good choice. Carpet needs to be of a rot-resistant and washable type, and carpet tiles may be suitable.

Hall

The hall is the first part of a home that visitors see, where they get their first impression of the residents and the way they live. For this reason, many families feel that a well-proportioned hall is important. On the other hand, this is space, like the landing, that has to be heated and cleaned but cannot be counted as part of the living accommodation unless it's big enough to be used for another purpose (see open plan, p. 13). At the very least, space is needed for family and visitors to take off coats and hang them up before going into a living room.

If the stair goes straight up from the hall, which is the commonest arrangement, it's important that the front door should be well draught stripped or protected by a porch.

Glass entrance doors let light into a hall, and can let you see who's at the door, but they're liable to let your callers see rather a lot of you, too. They're also vulnerable to burglars, especially if they're not in plain view from the road. There should *always* be a rail across the middle of a glass door, especially if it's at the foot of stairs, unless the pane is of toughened glass. Some of the most horrifying accidents involve people falling through panes of glass.

Porch

As I said above, an enclosed porch is very valuable for keeping heat in. It also provides somewhere for visitors to wait for the bell to be answered and for the milkman to leave the milk.

There should be a bell, and either a nearby streetlamp or a special light. Letterboxes should be high enough to use without stooping and large enough to devour magazines without chewing them.

There is some danger of leaks where the porch joins the wall.

In some districts the back entrance is usually used, the front entrance being reserved for the most formal occasions. If so, the back door should have porch, light and bell, and should lead to the hall rather than into the kitchen.

In modern housing, where there is separate access on one side of the houses for cars and on the other for pedestrians (marvellous for children), both entrances may be of equal importance.

Garage

Garages built into houses should have been properly fire-proofed, because petrol is a serious fire hazard. The wall should be at least a half-brick one, and any connecting door has to be solid (it will feel heavy), have a self-closing spring, and a frame with deep rebates (25 mm/1 in). Having such a door is very convenient, because it makes the garage useful for storage for everything from pram to vacuum cleaner, garden tools, fishing tackle and so on.

Not all garages are big enough for all cars, and double garages which take cars one behind the other aren't very convenient, for obvious reasons.

Heating

Most people would expect the whole of a house to be centrally heated nowadays, and would think unheated accommodation an expensive extravagance. They want to be able to use every square metre of the home all year round.

Choice of fuel

'*Which?*' magazine regularly compares the costs of the various fuels available for space heating – read their latest report on this topic. The points which follow are general and cannot be related to variations in fuel prices.

Solid fuel Smokeless fuel is generally mandatory in towns.

For solid fuel there generally has to be a large fuel store and a brick chimney. These add considerably to the cost of the house when it is built and are almost impossible to add later. There will be dirty fuel to be moved and ashes to clear, though with modern appliances these chores are minimised. The main boiler may provide a visible fire as a focal point to a room.

18 **Gas** Gas is probably the most convenient, safe and economical

fuel. No storage is required, and there is no waste, but a flue is needed. This may be of the 'balanced' type, simply passing through an external wall.

Oil For oil a large storage tank is needed, and there have to be delivery and service pipes. A flue is needed. There are no chores – but oil has recently been among the more expensive fuels.

Electricity Electric heating is the least expensive to install, as neither a flue nor a store is needed. It is usually used with 'storage' installations.

Types of installations

The majority of heating systems work by circulating heated water round a building, though others use warmed air or point heaters.

Whatever the system, the installation should be able to raise the temperature by about 18°C, to maintain comfortable conditions when it's freezing outside. It might be necessary to add point heaters in exceptionally cold conditions (also useful on cool days outside the heating season). Proper controls are needed to avoid uncomfortably hot conditions. These can adjust both the output of the boiler and the performance of individual appliances, and may be supported by time clocks. Ideally, there should be one thermometer outside, recording the temperature there, linked to one inside which can be set to a predetermined temperature. The boiler is instructed by how many degrees it needs to raise the temperature, and sets itself accordingly. This can be made more sophisticated by having room thermostats, set to varying temperatures: these control not the boiler but the setting of, say, radiators in the particular room. In any case, it should always be possible to shut off the radiators or outlets in any individual room to conserve heat when accommodation isn't being used. You may find this last system described as 'thermostatic control' but this is a misnomer: it is only the set of controls which act automatically which should be described in this way.

Time clocks are also highly desirable, to turn the system on and off at predetermined times. Heating will come on before you wake or come home from work, and go off after you leave in the morning or go to bed.

In flats, the controls may be such that you can shut the whole system or part of it off to suit your own convenience, or the block as a whole may be heated. In the latter case you might find you have to pay for heating whether you want it or not.

Circulating hot water Many heating systems depend on a heated supply of water which circulates around the building

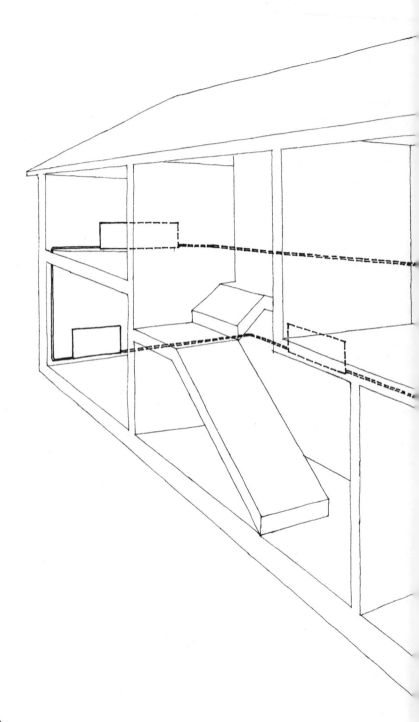

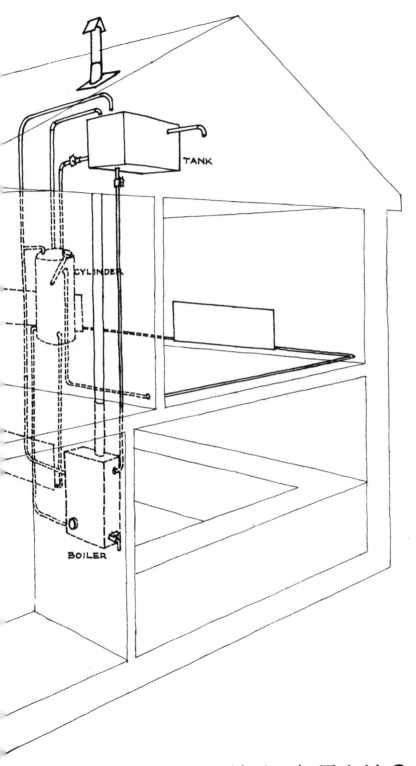

TANK

CYLINDER

BOILER

through pipes. One common type, known as an indirect system, is shown in the drawing: you will see that a small quantity of water circulates through the ·boiler and cylinder where it heats a larger quantity which circulates around the building.

The circulations are provided with expansion pipes, because heated water expands and could burst the system unless there is some kind of safety valve. These discharge over the same tanks from which the supply is drawn. Other safety devices include stop taps and overflows.

Such a system is simple and well-tried. Providing the pipes and tanks are well lagged where no heat is needed, this is an efficient means of heating, and virtually any kind of fuel can be used. The major disadvantage is that the pipes and radiators are bulky and make arranging furniture difficult. Modern systems have pipes about 25 mm (1 in) in diameter, and steel radiators which are flat and rather large in area. Water circulation is assisted by an electric pump, which means the household is at the mercy of electric cuts, whatever fuel is used for heating.

To get rid of obtrusive pipes, one variation involves hot water circulating through pipes embedded in the floor. The heat of the building's structure is raised and used as a reservoir. This is less responsive to changes in the outside temperature and therefore less efficient and more expensive to run.

Circulating air A system which circulates warmed (and sometimes humidified or cooled) air depends on a network of ducts built into the structure of the building. It isn't something you could install in an existing house, but it's an excellent system to find installed – responsive to outside temperature changes, pleasant because the air itself is heated, and unobtrusive. It is unlikely to be found in a pre-sixties building.

The boiler is rather bulkier than with a water-heating boiler, and incorporates filters (which need to be regularly rinsed) to ensure that the air isn't circulating dust. The fuel is usually oil or gas. The grilles through which the air reaches the rooms, and the return grilles at high level, should be unobstructed.

Storage heating The embedded coils described above are one kind of 'storage heating': they act by heating the structure, which in turn gives off heat through the day. There are two other forms of storage heating which use cheap off-peak electricity to work in a similar way.

Storage radiators These are large blocks of firebrick installed in convenient casings, which are heated up during off-peak periods and give off their heat when it is needed. The more sophisticated ones have adjustable grilles and fans to assist operation.

Underfloor heating Electric cables are embedded in the floor slab, in much the same way as the coils described above, to heat it. It is difficult to gain any control over heat output: any thermostatic control works from the overnight temperature, so that during a warm day that follows a cold night the house is liable to be uncomfortably warm, while during a cold day after a mild night it won't be warm enough.

Both systems are comparatively inexpensive to install, and storage heaters can be put easily into an existing building. Underfloor heating is particularly unobtrusive.

Point heaters In most homes it is necessary to supplement whole-house heating with point heaters for use in specially cold conditions or outside the main heating season. Whether these are fixed or mobile is a matter of preference but if you have gas in the house it is common to put in at least one fixed radiator or convector. A flue is essential. It's possible for such a fire to heat a back boiler – but you wouldn't want that to be your only summer source of hot water.

Solid fuel stoves You can have one of the excellent modern slow-burning stoves installed – these will provide hot water and also heat a few radiators. This involves a certain amount of dirty work in carrying fuel and ashes, but you may be prepared to put up with that for the pleasure of sitting round a real fire.

Arrangement The arrangement of pipes and radiators in a heating system clearly depends on the layout of the home. If proper care has been taken there should be short, well-lagged pipe runs, radiators placed on internal walls (so that heat leaking through the wall heats another space and not the garden), and the cylinder cupboard should be as near as possible directly above the boiler.

It is no longer considered mandatory to site radiators under windows, where a large part of the heat may be lost whenever the windows are open.

Thermal insulation Heating cannot be considered in isolation: good thermal insulation is equally important in providing comfortable conditions. This is dealt with on p. 34.

Cold water

Every water system, hot or cold, should be protected by a stop tap and a drainage point so that it can be emptied and worked on. There should also be a main stop tap to the entire installation on the rising main, often in a box with a hinged iron cover under the front path.

The cold water may be supplied direct from the main in the road (in which case the only storage tanks would be for the 23

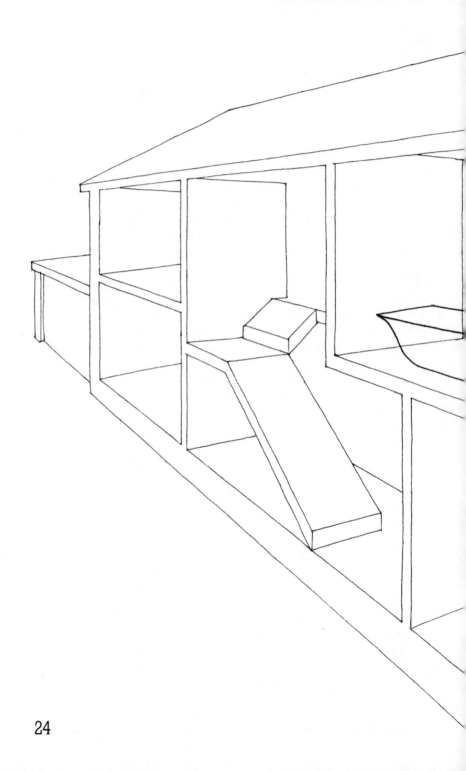

24

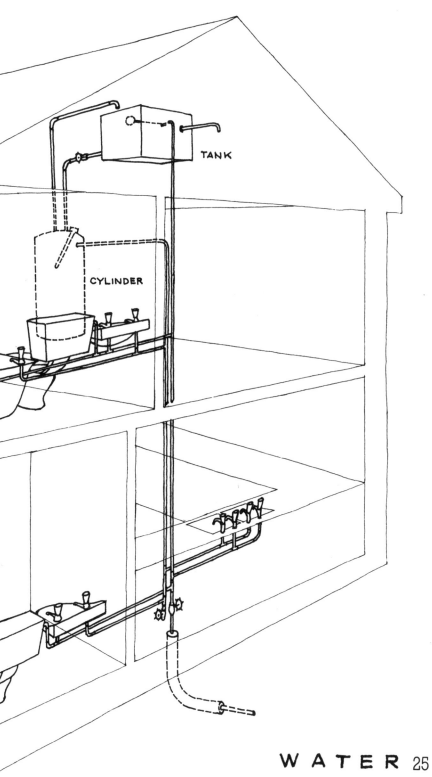

TANK

CYLINDER

W A T E R 25

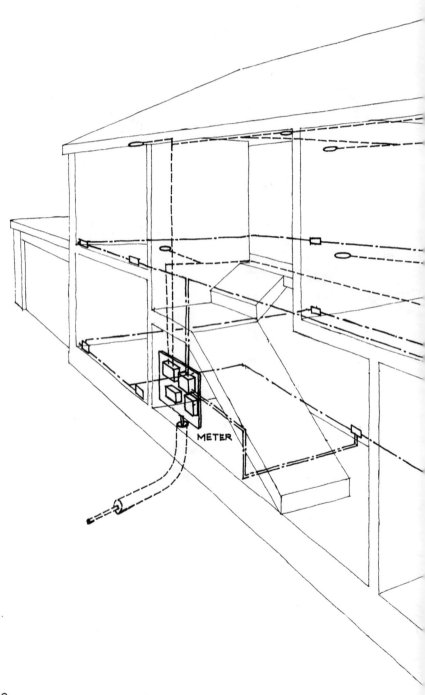

METER

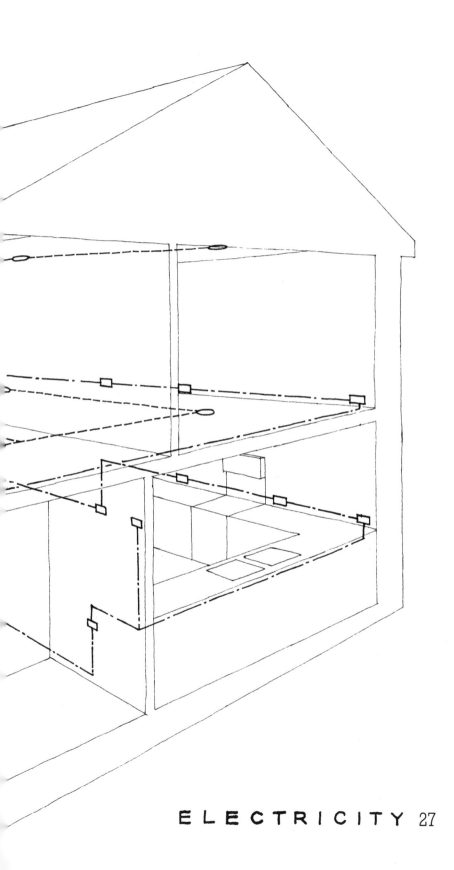

ELECTRICITY 27

heating and hot water systems, and for any blenders or showers); or the rising main may fill a storage tank, from which all the supplies (excepting perhaps a single drinking tap) are drawn. The water authority decides which system will be used in a particular district.

If cold water comes direct from the mains it will be at high pressure, pure and cool, but in emergency supplies are disrupted. If there is a tank it has to be big enough to hold a day's supply (90 litres or 20 gallons) for each person. The water will be at the same pressure as the hot water, so blenders, showers and mixers can be used.

All pipes, hot or cold, should be properly lagged and identified with coloured tags which cross-refer to a circulation plan prominently displayed.

Domestic hot water

The commonest way to supply hot water for domestic use is by a system on the lines of the one shown in the drawing, which is similar to the provision of hot water for heating (though separate from it).

The cylinder should be large enough to supply a full bath. For a large household allow 32 litres (7 gallons) per person. It should be very thoroughly lagged.

Hot water may also be supplied by storage heaters or instant heaters fuelled by gas or electricity. None of these is really satisfactory, though to supply extra water to a bedroom or cloakroom remote from the main circulation a small electric storage heater might be useful.

An electric storage heater is often installed to provide hot water from the cylinder when the main heating is off. This is particularly useful where the water is normally heated by a back boiler behind a room heater, but if the boiler is a modern one with selective controls it is generally more efficient to use that to heat water out of season than to resort to the use of an immersion heater.

Electric wiring

A modern system of electric wiring will include one or more ring mains for power. These are circuits designed to accept a maximum load on the assumption that not every socket outlet will be in use at the same time. They encourage the installation of adequate sockets, and the system is a safe and flexible one. In general, a system should provide enough outlets to avoid the use of adaptors, and they should be placed so as to avoid trailing flexes.

Wiring may be installed in conduit – round or oval tubes connected by junction boxes, through which the wiring is drawn – or by the use of cable insulated by lead (now uncommon), tough rubber or plastic. Wiring can be chafed and become brittle with age, so that all wiring should be checked after twenty-five years and every five years thereafter until it is renewed. Surface wiring in a house should, for appearance's sake, be covered with a fillet (a thin strip of wood), and it is good practice for all wiring to be accessible for renewal, though this isn't always the case.

The lighting circuits should allow for diffused lighting in most rooms – wall points, pelmet points and so on are better than a single ceiling point. Time switches can be used to control both power and lighting points: to use them on the lighting can be a useful burglar deterrent when you are away.

Drains

In principle, the wastes and drains which carry waste material from a house to the sewer system work by gravity and are designed to be self-cleansing and trouble-free. Details vary considerably, but all systems share two important features: the water trap, which is a bent pipe immediately below an outlet which holds water and so prevents sewer smells from getting into the property; the ventilation pipe, which rises above roof level and allows foul air to discharge where it will cause no nuisance.

The system is arranged so that every pipe is accessible for cleaning, and this is the purpose of the inspection chambers in the garden. Every length of drain can be cleared with drain rods from these points, in the case of a blockage.

Rain water may be carried away by the same system as the foul waste, may be allowed to soak away in a special part of the garden, can be collected in butts, or may be discharged into a separate set of sewers specially provided. The local authority decides which system is appropriate.

If there are no sewers reasonably accessible, a cesspit or septic tank may be used. The former is a sealed tank and needs emptying regularly, which is expensive. The latter is a small private sewage treatment plant, and needs emptying at less frequent intervals (perhaps six monthly against the fortnightly service needed by a cesspit). Either of these is perfectly sanitary. The local authority will direct the owner as to whether a cesspit or a septic tank is appropriate.

Gas

All gas appliances discharge fumes, and need proper flues, except for cookers and fridges which usually stand a little proud of the wall so that their fumes dissipate in the air of the kitchen.

Gas meters should not be sited in the same cupboard as electric meters unless there is a solid partition between them, because of the danger of a spark causing an explosion.

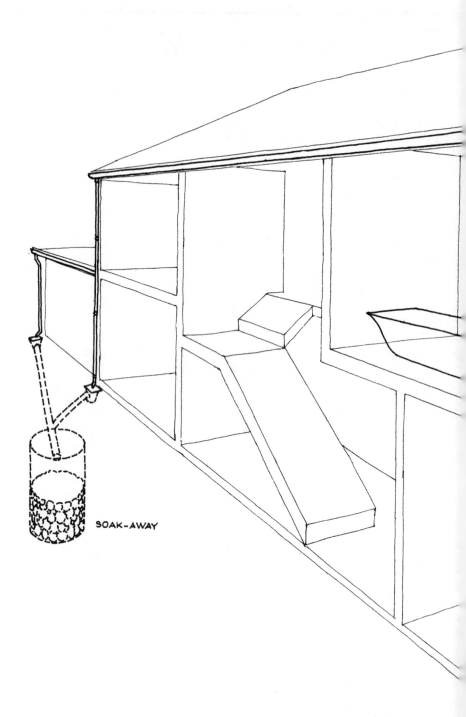

SOAK-AWAY

30

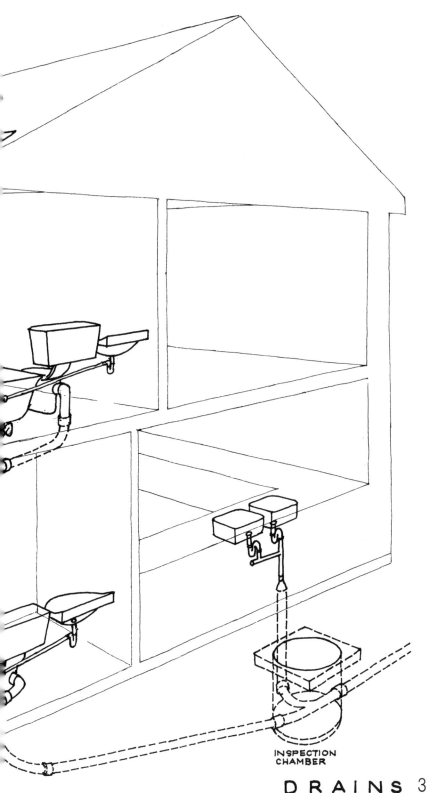

INSPECTION
CHAMBER

D R A I N S 31

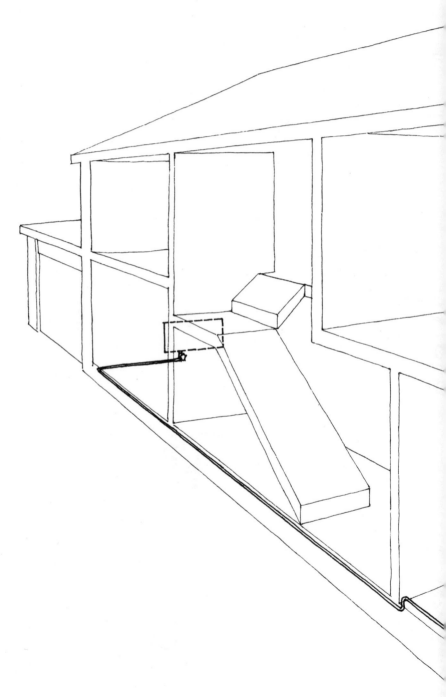

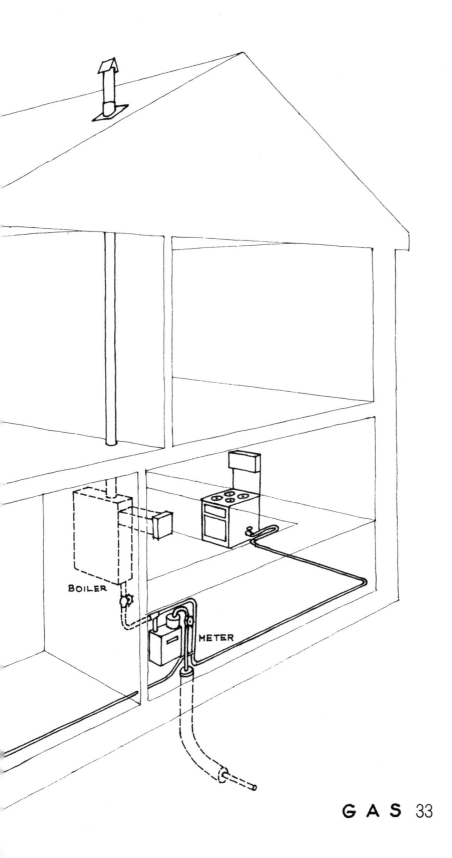

BOILER

METER

G A S 33

It is very convenient to have meters sited where they can be read without the householder being disturbed. This can be arranged (and often is, on modern estates) by housing the meters in a small box set into the outside wall, where there is a door to which the board has a key. Alternatively a small toughened glass panel covers the dials, so that the meter can be read without the door having to be opened at all.

Prepayment meters are very inconvenient.

Thermal insulation

The amount of heat which leaks out of a building through each square meter of its surface can be calculated from known characteristics of the materials from which it is made up: the figure obtained is the 'U-value', which is the generally used measure of the effectiveness of thermal insulation. It doesn't apply to a particular material, but to the whole assembly of materials that make up the thickness of that particular structure, so you might hear quoted the U-value of a cavity wall with brick on the outer face and an inner leaf of insulation blocks. The U-value of the windows, the roof, the floor and so on are all different, and to find the heat loss from a whole building it is necessary not only to know the U-value of each structure but what proportion of the building envelope is made up in that way.

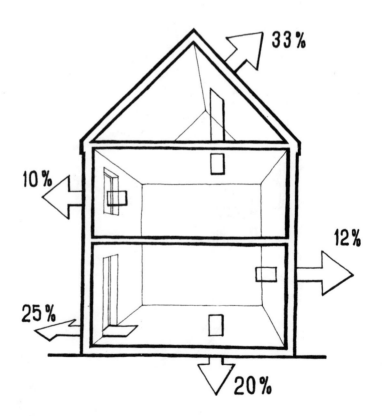

You might find that a third of the total was disappearing through the roof, 20 per cent through the floor slab and 25 per cent through gaps round doors and windows, leaving 12 per cent loss through the walls and 10 per cent through the windows. You will see, therefore, that double glazing which may be strongly advocated in promotional literature because it will more than halve the heat loss through windows, will in this case make only a small impact on heating bills, besides taking a very long time to pay for itself.

In Chapter 6 you will find guidance on what to look out for on thermal insulation when inspecting a building.

Sound insulation

The most important defence against unwanted noise comes from the planning of buildings. Living rooms that adjoin in semi-detached houses often cause trouble, whereas if the halls were together the problem wouldn't arise; in flats, living rooms next to the bedrooms of other homes can cause complaints. Note that noise within a household can be a problem, too – WCs next to bedrooms are specially troublesome. It is very difficult and expensive to improve the sound insulation of a building.

Chapter 6 suggests a strategy you could adopt if you suspect a noise problem.

2 Cottage or castle?

Do you hanker after the olde worlde charm of a country cottage, long to inhabit a leafy Victorian suburb or dream of a nice new house on a neat estate? Whatever your ideal, you must beware of letting its attractions blind you to its shortcomings. A castle may be damp and impossible to heat, a city centre flat could turn out noisy and cramped. In this chapter, I try to alert you to the main features of as many kinds of home as I can.

Older houses

Many people like the idea of a mature building, and some of the reasons are listed below, with comments to bear in mind.

Sound construction The widely held belief that 'they don't build like they used to' is in fact a *fallacy*. Older building is heavier, and better at keeping out unwanted noise, but otherwise inferior to modern construction. See p. 57 for a discussion of modern building techniques.

Space More rooms, for a large family or a wealth of hobbies. If this suits your lifestyle, remember that those extra rooms have to be painted, furnished and heated.

Larger rooms, to display furniture and to entertain, often appeal, but the extra space has to be carpeted, cleaned and heated.

High headroom is attractive to many people, but heat rises, so the extra space near the ceiling is the first to be heated. People who want a few well-sized rooms rather than a series of small ones are often best suited by a flat in a converted older house.

District A mature district with well-grown trees and nearer to the centre of town. A great deal of traffic may pass through the area, morning and evening.

Cost One can often buy more house for one's money if the property is older, but the yearly maintenance costs will certainly be higher.

Appearance Mellow materials, traditional looks – an entirely personal judgement.

Please read the description of the advantages of modern buildings which starts on p. 57.

36

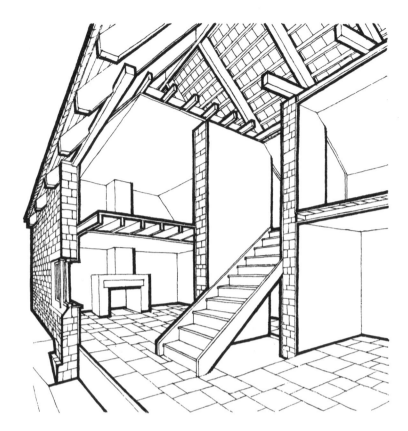

Country cottage

Let us look first at the planning and construction of the traditional country cottage. This is the basic dwelling type and evolved only slowly over the centuries. It was closely based on the life style of the occupants, the materials and skills of the locality and the prevailing climate. The accepted style of a district, once established, remained basically unchanged from the seventeenth century until the modern damp-proof course and cavity wall made it obsolete.

Invariably local materials – stone, brick, cob or timber – were used, and a local vernacular of details, refined by generations of craftsmen, may be peculiar even to a single village. This has two advantages: only devices that were found satisfactory in practice were retained, and the unity conferred by such consistency gives the village its charm.

Well-drained, sheltered sites on firm ground were chosen and walls were thick: there was no special damp-proofing, nor were foundations given much thought. White-washed lime plaster was the usual wall finish, and ground floors were laid directly on the earth and perhaps on flags.

Ceiling heights, particularly on an upper floor, if it existed, were low, and stairs generally went up directly from a ground floor room. Upper rooms were interconnected.

37

This outline tells you what to expect. You will of course carry out a rigorous inspection of the kind outlined in Chapter 6, paying special attention to points to which I have alerted you above. In addition, if you are seeking a cottage which has either been converted or with a view to conversion (and one or the other would usually be the case – few households would find the unconverted cottage I describe above habitable) you should note the specific points listed below.

Where a home is being chosen largely for its personality, the skill and imagination with which alterations have been made are crucial.

Check especially:

- Are any extensions that have been added in keeping in style, scale and construction? Have they been built to the standard of the Building Regulations? (Check this by asking at the building control department of the local town hall.)
- If windows have been put in to improve the lighting, do they spoil the outward appearance of the place?
- Has a damp-proof course been put in, and if so what kind is it? (See Chapter 8, p. 156 for the merits of the different types.) You are unlikely to get a mortgage unless there's a DPC, however dry the property seems to be.
- Is it drained to the sewer, or is there a septic tank or cesspit? The local authority will charge you for emptying either of the last two. If there is no proper drainage, you will have to put in

either a septic tank or a sewer (as the local authority directs) to their approval.

- Is there room in the kitchen for all the appliances you want? Is there sufficient kitchen storage? You are probably expecting less space than you would get in another type of home, but in this important area you don't want to have to cut your standard.
- Is the bathroom roomy enough for you?
- Have pipework and electric wiring been put in to professional standards? Are they neatly and unobtrusively arranged?
- Will the headroom really be adequate, even if you raise the floor to put in a DPC?

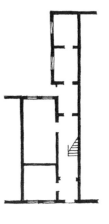

Eighteenth and early nineteenth century

In both town and country, medium-sized houses built before the middle of the nineteenth century were usually simply designed, tall, narrow and arranged in terraces. The architectural effect comes more from the terrace as a whole than from any particular striving for individuality: if one property has the stonework cleaned or puts in different windows it can spoil the whole terrace. The effect should be restrained and urbane.

Many such properties have been converted into flats which provide excellent homes with large rooms for small households. It is unfortunately difficult to get mortgages on such properties.

It isn't always easy to be sure of the date of a simple terrace house, but it can be helpful to note that towns and villages on the whole grew outwards, so the older properties are nearer the centre. Alterations and rebuilding, such as after bomb damage, can mean that knowing the age and how much of the place is original can be virtually impossible. It may be important, though, to be certain that what alterations have been made haven't weakened the structure. Your surveyor should be asked specifically to report on this. See p. 102.

In the London area, because of changes in the Building Acts which control construction, it is often possible to get a more accurate date than in the provinces. For example, parapets rather than wooden cornices where roof and wall meet came in with an act of 1707, and a four-inch recess to windows from the outside face of the wall with one of 1709.

It may also be helpful to know that London stock bricks were red up to the end of the eighteenth century, when the familiar yellow colour first appeared.

Eighteenth-century drains were built of brick, and what we would regard as 'proper' drainage didn't appear until the 1860s.

Particularly in London, the road is built up above the general ground level, and the main entrance is arranged to be higher still and reached by a short flight of steps. Steps go down from the street to the basement, which is actually at garden level. This arrangement raises the main living rooms above the damp, and the basement was originally used for storage or a shop, although later on kitchens came to be planned there. The stair runs through a hall and landings off which are the rooms. There may be three or more upper storeys, with attics under the roof. If the house is 'single-fronted' there are usually three rooms at each level, while there are four or five in a 'double-fronted' plan. At first floor level a drawing room is often found, which is of double size, running through from front to back of the house. These arrangements are similar through many variations of size and in many different districts.

The floor to ceiling heights are often different on different floors, averaging around three metres, and the stairs to attics and basements may be steep and tortuous.

Houses during this period were very solidly built, with brick or stone external walls and thick, fireproof, party walls. During the earlier part of the period the main material was brick, while in the early nineteenth century this was covered with a fine, dense rendering ('stucco'). Good plasterwork and fine fireplaces are features of the interiors.

Timber in floor joists, roofs and stairs is generous, because before the scientific grading of timber big safety margins had to be allowed: creaking and noise transfer are not usually troublesome, but such timbers may, if not treated, be vulnerable to insect attack.

The weight of the very heavy roof and upper floors is carried on solid walls of standardized thicknesses, and the limits on timber lengths limit in turn room sizes, so that even very large houses tend to have narrow rooms. The walls are pierced by vertical windows so as not to weaken them too much, leaving enough masonry to carry the load down to the heavy foundations which distribute it evenly over the ground.

Windows are almost always double-hung sashes, in which both the top and bottom sections slide vertically and are counterbalanced by weights. Later houses have the boxes in which the weights run concealed in the wall thickness. You may find 'crown' glass, which shows *faint* concentric rings – beware of obvious 'bottle' glass which is almost always bogus. Internal shutters are prized, but alas subject to rot.

Other features which improve the value of a property include panelled doors (which, though of hardwood, were usually painted – it isn't appropriate to strip any but the grandest), bolection moulds, simple porches (especially shell hoods in grander houses), and fanlights over entrance doors. All of these are common features of Georgian houses.

Pretty wrought iron balconies, elliptical arches, arched windows, arches as features of the wall surface, bow fronts and stucco are features of the Regency.

The roof may be rather flat, and covered with lead, or, in earlier houses, steeper and slated.

When it was built, the house might have had a pumped water supply in the basement, and main drainage in towns, but that would be the limit of the amenities. This means that any house you inspect will have had services put into it since it was built, and how well or badly this was done is important to the value of the house. Though rooms were usually well proportioned in the first place, this can be ruined by clumsy alterations. Whether you are looking at a total conversion into flats or at less major alterations to put in bathrooms, you should look carefully for cornices which don't go all the way round ceilings, for rooms which are too tall for their shape and for windows that are badly placed, all of which are among the effects that ill-thought-out changes can have.

If you are seriously contemplating buying any property of this period you will need a meticulous survey made by a professional surveyor with special knowledge of the period (the Royal Institution of Chartered Surveyors will be able to recommend one). You may find that the building is 'listed', which will constrain the alterations that can be made to it.

You can, however, decide for yourself whether it is worthwhile to go further into the matter. Check especially the following points, in addition to your normal inspection as set out in Chapter 6.

- Number of floors. Can you cope with all those stairs?
- Ceiling heights: expense of heating, expense of decoration, adds to stair heights.
- Type and condition of windows. Do sashes open? Are the sash cords in good condition? (Note that if cords have to be renewed, the boxes have to come off, which involves repainting the windows.)
- Is the plasterwork original? Is it in good condition? It is expensive to repair.
- Are there original stairs, balustrades, balconies, crown glass, panelling, fireplaces – any of which would add to the value?
- Is the timber sound? See Chapter 7. Look especially for signs of insect attack in the roof timbers and of fungal attack in panelling, behind shutters and in fittings, but be generally and particularly alert to the chance of decaying timber throughout your inspection.

Most homes in this type of property need something doing to them, and for that local authority permissions will be needed. This is dealt with in Chapter 9, p. 174, but there is one point I should like to make here. It is possible to find that you have to do more work than you want to undertake. This is because the authority is entitled to insist that the whole property is brought up to the standard of the building regulations when *any* application for approval is made. They might insist on a damp-proof course being added, for example, or 150 mm (6 in) of 'oversite' concrete being put over the entire ground area under the building. It's not usual for them to insist on every particular of the regulations being met, but they would normally expect the building to be put into what they regard as a fit state.

Early Victorian (1832–1878)

Medium- to large-sized Victorian houses often seem pretentious to modern eyes, particularly in comparison with the restrained elegance of the beginning of the century. The simple plan shape has often given way to a labyrinthine multiplicity of smaller rooms, each intended for a particular purpose, which naturally have to be approached by convoluted passageways. In those days, of course, there was ample help to run the household, but such properties can nowadays be tiring and time-consuming to live in.

Ceiling heights remain high, and the basement (usually accommodating the kitchen) continues to be a regular feature.

Such properties can best be recognised by the robust decoration with which they were embellished. Plasterwork, porches, window surrounds, fireplaces and other features are in a bold version of either a classic or a 'gothick' style. The detail can seem overbearing, but other stylistic details which are prized include moulded ceramic floor tiles, faïence lintols and other 'dressings', pretty bargeboards and porches, and wooden or cast-iron conservatories.

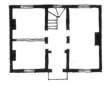

Not all such houses are excessively large, and they are generally well built, though lacking damp-proof courses. Look for walls one-and-a-half bricks thick, which will reasonably resist the penetration of driving rain (though less effective than a modern cavity wall). Walls thinner than this would be very vulnerable to damp. You will probably have to put in a damp-proof course if this hasn't already been done.

It is easier to insert bathrooms and kitchens into these houses than into earlier ones, because of the peculiarities of the plan.

Check especially, in addition to your detailed inspection as suggested in Chapter 6, the following points:

- Damp in the basement. Is there a proper damp-proof course?
- Creaking floor boards. Occasionally there has been cheese-paring over timber.
- How long ago was the house wired for electricity? Does it need rewiring?
- Are there more fireplaces than you need? Do you want to retain them as features (there may be one in every room)? 43

- Check the condition of decorative features. Removal would damage the house, but repair could be costly.
- Pay particular attention to the district, especially to signs of a deteriorating district or one that's on the rise. (See Chapter 5, p. 93.)

Late Victorian (1878–1900)

At this point we enter the realm of soundly constructed but largely unpretentious houses that are likely to make good modern homes without too much expense. Foundations, oversite concrete and damp-proof courses should all be present, at least in London; plans are simpler and the style of decoration, with romanticised 'gothick' detail on porches and so on, is one most of us can enjoy.

Whether the structure is of brick or stone, or merely faced with stone, the walls are usually solid but sufficiently thick to discourage damp from getting through. Although the introduction of the damp-proof course led fairly quickly to the

abandonment of basements, dry commodious ones which can readily be converted into comfortable living space are found. Look for a damp-proof course which consists of two courses of blue bricks or slates, not the modern thin-sheet material.

Room sizes are generous by modern standards – Victorian furniture was massive – and headroom around 2·6 m (8 ft 8 ins) is common. This is high enough to seem airy, without being excessively expensive to heat or demanding overlong stairways.

Features include stained glass, which is much prized. Especially admired is the 'flashed' type, in which a coloured layer of glass is cut away from a clear backing in decorative patterns.

Water and drains may be untouched from the time of construction – take care to check them. Be especially sure that there are no lead water pipes and that the drains are clear.

Early, original bathroom fittings are much admired, especially boxed-in baths and decorated WCs.

Gardens tend to run to damp shrubbery, full of gloomy laurels: but gardens aren't hard to alter.

The beginnings of the 'suburb' can be seen at this time, with small two-storey houses, each in its own plot. They often have long narrow gardens, and these may be served by a passageway at the bottom. It may be impossible to find room for a garage.

Larger houses from this period may be particularly suitable for cooperative ownership, because there are a number of good-sized rooms and the halls are big enough to subdivide if that's needed.

Early purpose-built flats from the later nineteenth century are either tenements with very limited facilities or fairly opulent 'mansion' blocks. These may have fireplaces and flues, second stairways, and the shared spaces are usually spacious. They are almost entirely restricted to the London area.

Some of the best bargains on the market are unmodernised houses of this period, especially artisan terraces, which can be turned into beautiful small homes, often on a do-it-yourself basis. It's critical to check the neighbourhood if you have this in view.

For all property in this group, in addition to your normal checks as described in Chapter 6, check especially:

- The services. If they're original they probably need attention.
- The condition of all woodwork in fascias, bargeboards, windows. It is often decayed through poor upkeep of paintwork.
- That the damp-proof course is working.
- Can you get your car off the road?

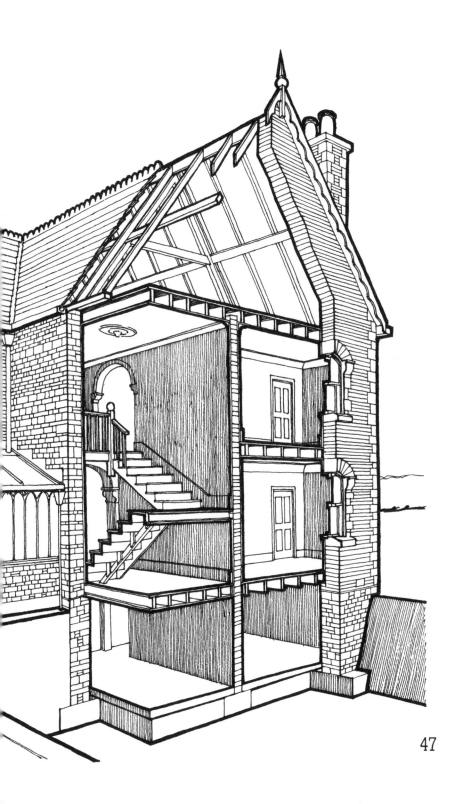

Edwardian (1900–1914)

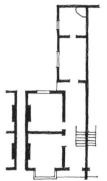

This was a period of great self-confidence, and there is a wide range of sizes of house with similar characteristics. By the turn of the century, cellars and attics had practically disappeared. Many sturdy town villas were constructed with simple plans and rugged details. Typically of brick, with moulded faïence trim and with ceramic tiled floors to halls, such houses may seem rather small for the imposing stairs and fireplaces they contain.

Terraced or semidetached houses are often arranged with an entrance hall leading to an inner hall (sometimes, but not always, through doors) which leads to the stair and to two living rooms of approximately equal size. There may, even in a modest house, be a back hall with a door to the yard between the hall and the kitchen. The kitchen is often supplemented by a scullery or wash house, with another outside door. This keeps the kitchen cosy and provides space to convert the scullery to a modern kitchen and the kitchen to a dining room.

Upstairs, two double and one single bedroom had become the norm and there would usually be a proper bathroom with WC and geyser. There may not be daylight on the landing.

The external walls of such houses are usually solid, but it's always necessary to check the thickness – around 300 mm (12 in) is about the minimum that's likely to be watertight.

Slated roofs are common and they are usually sound. The timbers are still big enough to allow for some decay without collapsing, but if ceilings appear to be sagging the support should be checked.

Bay windows are a common and distinctive feature and need a sceptical glance. They add floor space but do nothing to improve daylighting and, since their flat roofs can carry a load of snow which may be melted by escaping heat, they are vulnerable to damp. Look for damp stains on the decorations over the opening. Occasionally, too, the foundations of bays are shallower than those of the house, with resulting differential settlement. Porches are similarly suspect.

Typical features include stained glass, frosted glass to bathroom windows, ceramic sinks, large larders and mirrored overmantles.

Such houses may be especially attractive to purchasers who want to work from home, since there are likely to be one or two spare rooms; to large families; and to people with space-demanding hobbies.

Check especially, besides your normal inspection, as described in Chapter 6:

- Signs of damp around projecting features.
- The thickness of external walls.
- Sagging ceilings.
- The surroundings and district (see Chapter 5, p. 93).

Arts and crafts

During the later Victorian and Edwardian periods there was a move away from over-elaborate houses towards a much simpler style. At the same time as the houses I've described

above, homes of a quite different type were appearing. There are some at Bedford Park which date from 1876, at Port Sunlight from 1888, and at Bournville from 1894. They are part of a tradition of 'garden suburbs' which continued to affect thinking about houses up to quite recent times.

The houses are set out informally, often singly or in semidetached pairs, and have gardens round them. There is a conscious effort to get away from 'classic' or 'gothic' ornament, and what decoration there is is likely to be in the 'art nouveau' style. They can be recognised from their overhanging eaves, sweeping gables, hipped tiled roofs and casement windows.

The style also introduced more profound changes. As well as tending towards lower ceiling heights, houses began to be 'organically' planned. That is to say, the plan derives more from the style of life of the residents than from the method of construction adopted. Open planning begins to be found (though it wasn't common until the widespread adoption of whole-house heating) and rooms vary more in size than hitherto.

Such houses may be found in the suburbs of many towns. With the addition of modern heating and kitchen fittings they are very well adapted to modern life, especially of families with children. They appear to have popularised the 'french' window.

There are few points in addition to those listed in Chapter 6 to which you should pay particular attention, but check especially:

- Kitchen size: will it house modern appliances?
- Garage access and space.
- Thermal insulation: these houses date from before modern standards of insulation were introduced, and if open-planned may be very expensive to heat.

Flats

Flats converted from other properties

Many Victorian houses which are now too big for a single family are split up into several homes. This has been done in some other types of building, too, such as redundant schools or warehouses. As well as extending the useful life of the building, this can, if done sympathetically, make individual flats with large rooms, a pleasant entrance and a spacious site. These may attract retired people, and there are schemes deliberately aimed at them, where some shared facilities (perhaps a restaurant) and the presence of a manager, and a cooperative maintenance arrangement are included. On the other hand, if it's done without sufficient care the result may be badly proportioned, ill-arranged rooms, crudely added kitchens and escape stairs, and badly maintained shared areas.

The distinction between a flat and a maisonette is rather obscure. Generally it means shared access for a flat and independent access for a maisonette.

It is very important to look not only at the flat you are considering buying but also at the state of the whole building. If other owners let their property deteriorate this will affect the value of everyone's home.

As well as inspecting the flat as you would any other property of similar date, make sure you understand the overall layout of the building. It may not be immediately obvious that your bedroom is next to the toilet of the flat next door, or that your living room is over someone else's bedroom so that you'd have to be constantly careful not to disturb neighbours.

A further vital point is to understand the arrangements for looking after shared areas. In some cases a service charge is paid to cover this, while in others the owners work out a rota for doing the work themselves. This is only satisfactory if everyone pulls their weight.

Some conversions have been successfully carried out on the basis of shared ownership of the entire property. A group of like-minded people buy a suitable building and either commission alterations or plan the work on a do-it-yourself basis to provide tailor-made accommodation for each household. They foot all the bills on a strictly pro rata basis, and usually the ownership remains with a specially set-up company of which they are all shareholders. When anyone wants to leave they sell their shares rather than the particular flat. A big advantage is that the whole property is maintained to an agreed standard.

Converted flats are, I'm afraid, unpopular with building societies, but may be a good investment for retired people who want to avoid the responsibility of maintaining a building and garden, and have their own capital.

Purpose-built flats

Older purpose-built flats are generally steel-framed or brick buildings four or five storeys high, if there are lifts, or on three floors if they depend on stairs. Flats have a long history – there were ten-floor tenements in Edinburgh as long ago as the sixteenth century.

It's very important to be sure that the plan is arranged so that the bedrooms of one flat are not arranged next to the living room of the one next door or above or below. Soundproofing may be better than you'd find in a modern block, but it's wise to check how much of a nuisance noise would be.

Heating in older blocks may burn solid fuel (inconvenient on upper floors) or electricity (which is expensive).

It is vital to look at the way in which the shared areas are kept up and at the costs of service schemes.

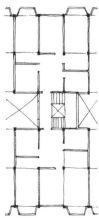

Flats of this type are an excellent choice for groups of friends sharing a purchase, especially if they have little wish to keep up a garden. They may be suitable for retired people, if the lifts are reliable. They are only suitable for families with small children if there are private gardens and someone with the time to supervise play there.

A major advantage to many households may be that flats of this type are concentrated in inner suburban areas with excellent access to city facilities. They are much commoner in London than in the provinces.

Interwar period (1918–1939)

The period between the wars was notable for the great improvement in public transport – the metropolitan railway, for example – and for the spread of the building society movement, accompanied by the ambition for house ownership. These two developments produced a burst of housebuilding and the sprawl of most of our industrial cities.

The depression, however, had a serious effect on standards of building, since economy became a priority, and many houses from this period are less soundly constructed than those of either earlier or later date.

The wartime Tudor Walters Committee had reported in favour of three-bedroomed, two-storey houses, and these became almost universal, with great emphasis on semi-detached property. Houses were very repetitive, but there was, nonetheless, more attention paid to the individual dwelling than to the block, as opposed to earlier terraces.

The interwar house provides a high proportion of our housing stock, but unfortunately has a number of deficiencies. The cavity wall did not become universal until the late thirties, and many of these properties have one-brick walls which may be defective in damp proofing and thermal insulation. Often they are covered (sometimes only in part) with coarse renderings, such as roughcast or pebbledash, which demand considerable maintenance, and panels between windows may be quite simply of tile hanging or weatherboarding on a timber framework or 'studding' with no more than a lath-and-plaster inner lining.

The rooms are often small, and have been planned to a set area with little attention to the space requirements of furniture. The typical three-bedroom semidetached house has two living rooms of roughly equal size and a kitchen which is small by modern standards. Upstairs, there is a small bedroom over the kitchen, and the bathroom is over the entrance hall, so that service runs are lengthy.

The back door usually enters the kitchen without a back hall. There is a fuel store and a small larder (often under the stairs) but no space provided for the dustbin.

Originally the hot water will have been provided from a back boiler (very occasionally from an independent boiler in the kitchen) behind one of the living-room fires (or the cooking range in the north), and there would be fireplaces in the two larger bedrooms. There would be gas and an adequate electrical installation for the time, though not for modern needs.

There is generally just enough space between adjacent houses for a single shared driveway, and if there are two garages served from this they obstruct the narrow garden. The typical plot is very long and narrow.

The roof is normally tiled, hipped, gabled and without insulation.

Thirties houses are very difficult to convert or modernise and inconvenient to live in. They lack space where this is most needed and tend to have been cheaply built to standards that would not be acceptable today. However, there are exceptions, and the slightly larger houses allow some scope for imaginative adaptation. Exchanging the function of dining room and kitchen (see p. 173) often works well. The smallest interwar houses may be bought relatively cheaply and may offer a rewarding challenge to a household prepared to devote energy and imagination to their conversion. A first-time buyer might find this a good entry point to the house market.

In addition to the normal checks listed in Chapter 6, check especially:

- Size of kitchen: will the appliances go in?
- That your furniture can be sensibly arranged in the rooms.
- Headroom on stairs, for getting furniture up. It is often minimal.
- Hot water and heating services.
- That there's room to get your car to and into the garage.

International style (1920–1939)

In the same way as the 'Arts and Crafts' movement ran parallel with late Victorian and Edwardian design, so the ideas of the functionalists influenced avant-garde designers in the twenties and thirties without disrupting the evolution of the house.

At this time, architecture was released by the development of the reinforced concrete frame from the tyranny of load-bearing structures, and on the continent houses began to be built with free-flowing enclosed space designed to suit the functions required of them. Corbusier said that a house was a machine for living in, and the aim was to design a perfect machine.

Reinforced concrete meant that there could be very large window openings, that windows could be at or actually go round corners, and that roofs would usually be flat. Reinforced concrete presented a bland white appearance.

A few genuinely modern houses were built in Britain between the wars, but you are unlikely to be offered one of them. They change hands for very high prices. More properties which seized on the stylistic motifs of the flat roof, corner window and white wall were built. Essentially these are no different in layout and construction from other houses of the period, except that the roofs may be prone to leaking – the covering is now old – and that rendering is always somewhat suspect. The new technology that could make bent glass was exploited in the corner windows: these panes are expensive to replace.

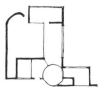

In addition to the normal content of your inspection on the lines set out in Chapter 6, check especially:

- That the roof is watertight.
- That renderings are sound.

Immediate postwar (1945–1961)

Directly after the war, stringent controls operated on all building work, and there were limits both on the size and the cost of houses. Many houses were deliberately designed for later extensions, and in some cheap materials were deliberately chosen to be replaced later. The intentions of the original builders have not always been fulfilled.

Plans remained very similar to the prewar pattern, though shortages of materials, and money, led to some cheap substitutes being employed and some sophistications being omitted. There was usually a garage, but such features as hipped roof or decorative gable are rare. Flat roofs and curved windows do not appear.

In addition to the normal inspection, outlined in Chapter 6, check especially the following points:

- Floor tiles to solid ground floors are firmly stuck down.
- Kitchen size and arrangement suit your needs.
- Roof insulation.

Prefabricated houses

During the aftermath of the war, large numbers of prefabricated houses which were intended to be temporary were put up round our cities. Most have now disappeared or outlived their purpose, but some are still in use.

You should remember that these houses showed a considerable advance in standards at the time they were built, having central heating and fitted kitchens. They were built, however, of materials which were at the time unconventional.

When inspecting a house of this type, look especially at two points additional to the normal checks:

- Be alert to any sight of rust, especially at junctions and joints of the exterior cladding panels.
- Inspect all joints and fastenings to ensure they are sound.

Modern construction

There's a widespread belief that modern construction is poor and that the older the building the better built it will be. This couldn't be further from the truth. I think it is based on memories of some fairly disastrous 'jerry building' that went on between the wars, which was inferior to previous standards. However, modern building achieves standards undreamt of previously, and is continually improving. For this we can thank the evolving building regulations, which encapsulate and

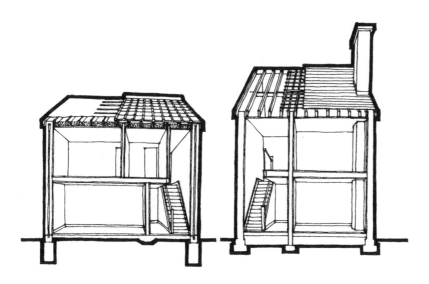

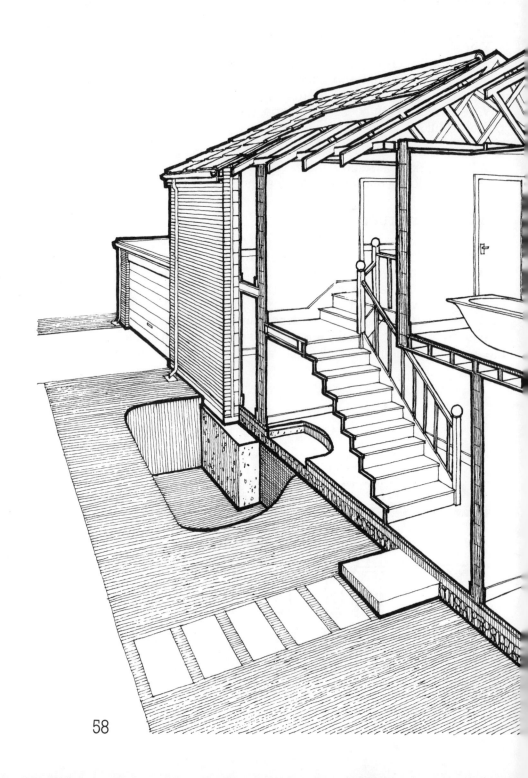

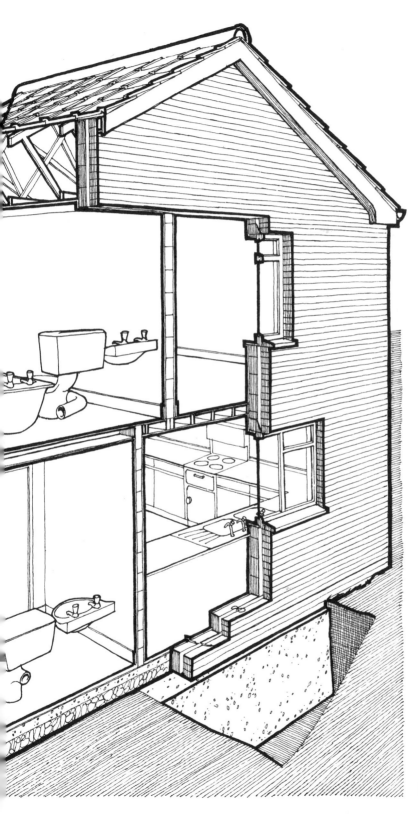

59

enforce the best of available practice, and the extensive research programme carried out by governmental and other bodies.

We are able to use slenderer and lighter materials today, so that loads on walls and foundations are reduced, we have watertight rather than water-resistant walls, we have completely watertight damp-proof courses, and we expect and attain high standards of thermal insulation.

In addition, the services installed in houses are comprehensive, and heating and power require little or no attention. Every part of the building has been carefully planned to be useful, and if space is limited, it is used to the full.

Modern methods of house construction are economical of materials and labour, provide high environmental standards and allow considerable freedom in planning. No doubt following years will see evolution as rapid as that of the past, as new materials and techniques become available: it is never possible to say that the ultimate in perfect construction has been attained, only that the best possible use is being made of the resources at present available.

There is now far more emphasis on the combination of lightness and strength, and on the use of factory-made components: a high proportion of the parts assembled into a modern house has been factory-produced, which ensures consistent high quality and speed in construction.

Cavity wall
One extremely important advance has been the introduction of the cavity wall. By building the external walls of a house as two independent leaves, a complete barrier to the penetration of damp can be created without loss of strength. The outer leaf is of facing bricks chosen for their appearance, while a load-bearing insulation block is chosen for the inner leaf. The leaves are connected by galvanised steel ties, from which any water which might penetrate the outer leaf would drip down the cavity. At edges, such as window openings, great care has been taken by introducing a layer of damp-proof material to ensure that no path for water is created.

Cavity walls are almost universal in postwar houses.

Foundations
The foundations are often deeper than those of earlier properties. They are, therefore, much less likely to be affected by frost. The load of the building has also been greatly reduced, so that foundation failures are very rare. A modern foundation may have the whole trench filled with concrete, which is cheaper than the labour-intensive brick footings found previously.

Alternatively, and especially where the load-bearing capacity of the ground is thought suspect, the building may be supported on a comparatively shallow raft of reinforced concrete. Differential settlement is then most unlikely to occur.

Precautions against damp

In modern buildings there is invariably a positive barrier to the upward passage of ground water in the form of a damp-proof course of impermeable material. This gives much more positive protection from rising damp than the reliance on using only well-drained sites of all periods up to the late nineteenth century. It is incorporated in the walls a minimum of 150 mm (6 in) above ground, and no higher than the level of the lowest floor, thus causing the universal step up into buildings. Often a complete layer of damp proofing covers the whole floor area today, across the mandatory 150 mm (6 in) layer of oversite concrete, and protected by a layer of fine concrete on which floor tiles are laid. Both the damp-proof course and this latter damp-proof membrane are usually of heavy black polythene.

Ground floors

The oversite concrete has to be put into all buildings, as a protection against plants and, to some extent, damp. Sometimes it lies beneath a suspended floor of joists and boards, supported on honeycomb 'sleeper walls', but often on level sites it forms the floor itself, being covered by hardwood blocks, plastic tiles or carpet.

Upper floors

Upper floors are supported by joists in the traditional way, though because of modern grading techniques and the ability to calculate the strength of members accurately, the joists are light by older standards. These carry a covering of boards, or perhaps of chipboard, which provides a good level base for carpet.

Partitions

Partitions, particularly upstairs, are more often made of a timber frame covered with plasterboard and a thin 'skim' coat of plaster. These reduce the load on the foundations and are therefore beneficial, and it is easy to attach fittings to them and conceal electric wiring in them.

On the lower floor some partitions are probably load-bearing, and these will be built of blocks similar to those used in the inner leaf of external cavity walls, though not precisely the same.

Stairs

The staircase usually arrives on site as a complete unit, and is 61 simpler and firmer in construction than in earlier periods. The central carriage you would find in an earlier stair is usually absent, but the treads and risers are carefully framed into the strings which support them.

Roof

The roof structure generally consists of an intricate framework of light members, fixed together with metal connectors, which support the rafters, battens and tiles. There should be a felt underlay, known as 'sarking', over the rafters and under the battens, to carry any water which blows under the tiles down to the gutter. The tiles are most usually of an interlocking type which reduces the need for a big overlap and so lightens the roof. If there is a chimney, it may be designed so that the chimney breast projects outwards instead of interrupting the roof (with the added advantage of not interrupting the floor space indoors), but wherever the roof comes up against a higher structure there will be lead flashings rising 150 mm (6 in) above the roof surface and tucked into masonry joints to waterproof the joint between wall and roof.

The two big advances in roof design are the striking decrease in weight due to interlocking tiles and modern framing techniques, and the improvement in thermal insulation. There should be 100 mm of fibreglass quilt or loose fill between ceiling joists.

Windows

In the immediate postwar period galvanised steel windows with small panes vied for popularity with wooden ones, but since the end of the fifties wood has been much the more common. The sizes of windows are standardised, and so are the sections from which they are constructed: though specially designed windows can be had, it is unusual for these to be used in houses. Aluminium, which needs minimal maintenance, has recently come into fairly widespread use for windows in private homes.

Double glazing has been incorporated into many better-class houses built since the mid-sixties.

It has taken many years to develop window sections which shed the water and discourage its penetration into the building, and the adoption of such sections is an obvious benefit.

Window cills are usually of wood, and the window boards (often wrongly called cills) on the inside of the window may be of wood or tile.

Doors

The doors of modern houses are almost invariably of flush construction. A lightweight but very strong core is covered on both sides either with hardboard (which provides the best surface for painting) or plywood (which polishes well). The use of modern adhesives results in strong, durable doors of limited weight. Their frames are usually, internally at least, simple linings to the openings, to carry the hinges, and the opening is trimmed with architraves.

Structure
New materials which are notably consistent in quality, as well as increased understanding of older ones, has made it possible for modern builders to be far more economical of resources than their earlier counterparts. The effect of this is cumulative. If the timbers of a roof are smaller, then the load which has to be carried by the walls is reduced, so that they can be less thick. In turn, less elaborate foundations are necessary, and so on.

In two respects, lighter constructions may have disadvantages. They transmit sound more than heavy ones, so that special attention has to be paid to sound insulation, and roofs need to be positively fixed down so that there is no risk of them being dislodged by the wind. Otherwise modern, light construction performs just as well as older, heavier methods. In many respects it is superior: we don't expect to find cracking due to failure of foundations, damp penetration through walls or rising damp in a modern building, but all are common in older ones.

Durability
Greater understanding of the chemistry involved in erosion caused by atmospheric pollution and similar mechanisms has led to these kinds of deterioration becoming less common. We know how to choose paints that will withstand sea air or industrial atmospheres, which materials should not be used together, and so on. The rigours of maintenance have in this way been minimised, and we are using more and more materials which demand little or no attention.

Environmental standards
It is in their ability to modify the external environment to produce acceptable internal conditions that modern buildings excel. By modern techniques water can be entirely excluded, windows can be shaped and positioned for optimum distribution of natural light, and very high standards of thermal insulation can be achieved. Even in the case of sound insulation (where, as I mentioned, problems may arise) freedom in planning and the ability to interrupt sound paths are available and helpful. Care is taken to avoid siting noisy areas near to quiet ones, and double windows and cavity walls are helpful.

Ventilation and humidity can be carefully controlled, services provide well-distributed and automatically managed heat and artificial lighting, while hot and cold water, drainage, power and gas are usually readily available. These services, because they are designed and installed as integral parts of the building, are economically laid out and unobtrusively sited.

Anyone buying an older house (for excellent reasons, discussed at the beginning of this chapter) has to accept that environmental standards comparable to those taken for granted today in a modern home may be difficult and expensive to achieve.

Modern estate house (1961–present)

This type of house forms the mainstream of modern homes.

The publication, in 1961, of the Parker Morris Report (*Homes for Today and Tomorrow*) had a great effect on the design of homes, and this date can therefore be regarded as a watershed.

The philosophy expressed in the report brought the overriding ideas of modern architecture into the realm of housing: the way the family wanted to use their home should be considered, the whole house should be heated, there should be well-considered storage, and so on. Instead of a gentle process of evolution governing the design of large numbers of houses, original thought began to be given to their arrangement and construction. Since the report was principally concerned with local authority housing, it was the design of public housing schemes which first benefitted. The effect reached the private house building sector eventually, how-

ever, and modern houses should be expected to be designed to accommodate the usual items of furniture, instead of simply having 'usual' room sizes, for example.

The degree of open planning to be found does vary from district to district across the country. In some areas this is popular, since it is felt to give a feeling of airy spaciousness, while in others it is disliked as interfering with privacy and demanding that the whole accommodation should be kept warm at all times. It tends, perhaps on account of the latter point, to be most popular with 'up-market' buyers.

Modern houses have excellent damp proofing, the damp-proof membrane being common, and a high standard of thermal insulation, and whatever the system of heating this should ensure that the whole house can be used at all seasons.

Plots on speculative estates are much smaller than was the case before the war, but this should not result in any loss of privacy where the houses have been carefully designed for their situation. An outdoor area sufficiently secluded and sheltered for meals to be taken should have been provided.

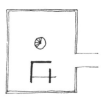

Purpose-designed houses

A house which has been designed and built for a particular occupant may display unconventional features. Whereas one

arranged to be suitable for the average' family may be generally adaptable to many uses, a purpose-designed one may be less amenable. It needs to be studied with special care against your own requirements. The special features which made it a worthwhile investment for its first owners may suit you well: on the other hand, they might make the house less suitable for you than a more conventional one.

If you feel that your requirements in a house, now that you've gone into them thoroughly, are specialised enough to warrant commissioning a tailor-made design, you should approach an architect straightaway (see Chapter 8, p. 152). Don't try to design your house yourselves: the architect is trained to interpret your needs, and will work more effectively and produce a better result if you give him your problem rather than a half-baked solution to it. One advantage of building is that you have more choice of site (subject to financial limitations and planning controls).

Purpose-built flats

Modern blocks of flats usually have reinforced concrete frames, which put severe limitations on the internal planning. They fall into two categories: there are high-density blocks (mainly in London) designed to make the best use of very expensive and desirable sites by arranging as many flats on the

area as possible, and there are more modest suburban groups, often not more than three storeys high, in which a number of small flats are combined into a single architectural 'statement'.

As local authorities have found, higher-density housing isn't necessarily achieved by building flats rather than houses. Higher buildings need to be further apart for decent light and ventilation. The increased cost of building high, and of maintaining lifts and service ducts, also makes flats relatively expensive.

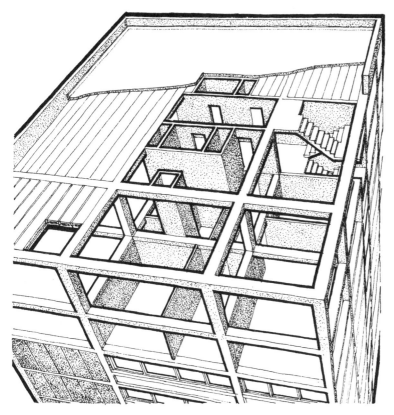

It's an interesting phenomenon that while tenants, especially local authority tenants, frequently complain about being 'herded' into flats, seeming to feel that this in some way dehumanises them, purpose-built flats are among the most sought-after homes for private buyers. The attractions of centralised maintenance and a convenient position outweigh, for them, any disadvantage in not being able to personalise one's home.

Two advantages of flats that are likely to attract buyers are that there is no garden to keep under control (though that does mean there's no outdoor living space), and the good appearance and prestige of the block. Busy career people are most likely to find these factors important, while families with children may have other priorities.

Internal layout

The planning is constrained by the need to place windows regularly, and the shapes and sizes of the room have to fit in with the structural grid imposed by the frame.

There tends to be a good deal of noisy intrusion from one flat into another, and in order to keep life reasonably civilised the residents generally have to subscribe to a set of rules to limit disturbance for everyone's benefit.

In some blocks services such as heating are provided centrally: it is essential to find out the arrangements for payment. If everyone pays a standard annual charge based on the area of the flat there is little incentive to economise (since one always feels that one is paying for other people's heat, and may as well get full value – which eventually maximises consumption). On the other hand, the individual metering of heat is itself expensive. Flats in the middle of the block tend to be kept warm by their neighbours even if they turn off their own system, so that some unfairness still creeps in.

There are often cooperative arrangements for cleaning, maintenance and repairs to the shared access areas, and in some schemes this extends to the whole property. This means that any need for repair is reported to a supervisor who makes the necessary arrangements. There may be an annual charge to cover this, or a separate bill may be sent (which keeps demands for maintenance within reasonable bounds).

Holiday chalet

Many houses built specifically as holiday homes show an exemplary use of space, though they may perhaps be too

confined for year-round comfort. Standards of insulation and weatherproofing should be high, as it usually is with modern prefabricated chalets. Not all of them, however, exhibit the high standard of security desirable in a house that may be left untenanted for long periods.

If you are considering buying abroad you must get help from both a solicitor and a surveyor with experience of the country concerned. In particular, never enter into a time-sharing agreement on overseas property without advice.

Unconventional construction

More and more houses are being built with timber frames, and are being found acceptable by building societies. Such construction is essentially sound, and relatively easy to provide

with a high standard of thermal insulation. It is essential that the external covering, which might be of brick, tiles, weatherboarding or plastic panels, should be truly weatherproof, and that the whole of the structural timber should have been pressure-impregnated with preservative before construction. You may find such a house difficult to recognise, since the appearance is little different from that of a conventionally constructed house. If the outer cladding material is other than

brick or stone, ask about the underlying construction – panels between windows, even in quite traditional houses, may be timber framed, as well as whole houses.

Some excellent modern prefabricated houses also exist though they don't often seem to come on to the market (perhaps their owners like them too much to leave). The advantages of complete factory production lie mainly in the high and consistent quality which can be maintained, since working conditions are so much more agreeable than those on a building site. There may be some advantages in speed of construction, which does not affect a second purchaser, and cost is comparable to that of a conventional house, similarly situated. Very high standards of insulation can be attained with factory-made components, which are reflected in decimated power bills.

Prefabricated buildings are generally recognisable because they are obviously put together out of parts, but it is a fallacy to believe that they all look the same. This is far from the case: while the early postwar prefabs were made with 'closed' systems, like an airfix model, it is more usual now for 'open' systems, more like lego, to be adopted, giving the designer at least as much scope for variety as can be achieved with bricks, tiles and standard windows.

The trend in the construction industry is now towards an ever-increasing amount of factory production. Stairs, doors, roof frames, as well as obvious fittings, are all standard units today. There is little doubt that this trend will accelerate rather than decline.

Single-storey houses

The term 'bungalow' was originally brought back from India by the Raj, and denoted a particular style of rather conventional, small, single-storey house. I prefer to call them all houses, however many floors they may have.

A single-storey house needs a bigger plot than a two-storey one, and as well as costing money in itself, this has the effect of increasing the lengths of roads and sewers and walking distances. Though more useful space can be planned into the area under the roof, because there is no space-consuming stair to accommodate, this does not mean that the house will be cheaper than a two-storey one. On the contrary, the extra expenditure on roof and foundations makes such houses potentially dear. Since they are also popular, especially with retired people, the price is usually yet further increased. You need to be sure that you know what premium you are being expected to pay because the house is on one storey and be certain that the extra money is worth it.

There are many excellently planned one-storey houses, but, because of the wider spans, ones with pitched roofs are not

always ideally arranged. Check this against your own requirements. Ones with flat roofs can be very well arranged indeed, but tend to have a great deal of external wall which must be well insulated. Look for a plan with a minimum of circulation space, rather than one arranged in a simple rectangular shape with long corridors.

Three-storey houses

Some superb houses have been built with garage and service areas on the ground floor, living areas on the first, and bedrooms on the second. An internal garage is almost always an advantage, since it is available for storage (providing fire

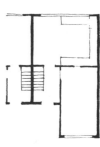

71

protection is properly taken care of, see p. 18). A problem, however, is that the living room is raised a floor above the garden so that the latter may not be much used, and parents may be reluctant to allow small children outside alone. The stairs can also be tiring.

Working homes

With the development of excellent means of electronic communication it is possible for more and more people to work from their homes. Were this line of development to continue, a very different light could be shed on our perception of a desirable residence. Although at present you may merely feel the need of a spare room to use as a study, it is possible that office blocks may become obsolete, and eventually be replaced by city-centre homes. This is not likely to have much relevance to present purchasers, except that it might affect the later value of their purchase.

Note that if you wish to work from home you may require planning approval, and will have to make sure there is no covenant that would prevent you from doing so (see p. 183). If you wish to claim tax relief on the use of part of your home as a workplace you may become liable to capital gains tax when you sell it.

Properties which have been altered

It is of course unlikely that you will find a property (unless it's brand new) which has never been altered in any way. Electricity may have been installed or rewired, central heating put in; new windows may have replaced old and rotten ones or the kitchen may have been modernised.

If such work has been done recently and on a generous scale, it can add considerably to the value of the property. If, on the other hand, it was done more than fifteen years ago it could be obsolescent – you may want to do it again soon. If, even worse, the job has been done amateurishly, you will be dissatisfied with it, and it would be better to buy a house or flat where you can start from scratch.

The worst case is where windows or other features have been added which are neither in character with the original building nor straightforwardly modern. 'Georgian' bow windows added to a Victorian house, for example. My instinct is to avoid such a property but if in every other respect it is ideal, and the price is low enough for you to afford to remove the solecism, you may find you have a bargain.

Value for money

A house is only worth the amount that *you* are prepared to pay for it: do not allow yourself to be persuaded that, because someone else has offered more, the place must be worth more to you. As you are very clearly aware, your needs are distinct from those of anyone else, and features which to you are disadvantages may be the very points which have endeared the house to another family.

Note, too, that space in itself isn't very valuable. It is only space which is well arranged for your particular purposes, which is light and well heated, ventilated and dry, which is worth paying for. Buying space for which you can see no use is unlikely to be a good investment. It will have to be maintained, rates will have to be paid on it – and all your junk will congregate there, instead of being discarded as it should be!

How old is it?

There are no hard-and-fast rules: details and features often appear both before and after the periods in which they are most common. However, there are some features of residential buildings at different times which may help you to tell the approximate age of one you're looking at.

Georgian

Areas of undecorated brickwork; slender sash windows, small panes; fan lights; windows regularly set out across the facade; elegant joinery; fine proportions; parapet hides flattish roof.

Regency

Stucco; bow fronts; elliptical arches; sash windows set out regularly across facade; parapet hides flattish roof; delicate wrought iron, especially balconies.

Victorian

Elaborate, intricate plans; conservatories; pointed roofs with eaves; heavy ornament, derived from classic design (fluted columns, cherubs) or from gothic design (pointed arches); ceramic floor tiles; sash windows. Note that the later the building the larger the panes of glass.

Edwardian

Brick dressed with stone or faïence; bay windows with sashes; elaborate fibrous plaster work; mirrored overmantles; built-in cupboards.

Arts and crafts

Irregular plan, sometimes with arches between rooms; varied room sizes; sweeping gables; hipped roofs; casement windows.

Interwar

Part external rendering, especially pebbledash; bay windows with gable over; solid walls; suspended ground floor, except to kitchen; scullery; several fireplaces; poor insulation.

Postwar

Documentary evidence of age should be available for any house of this period. However, as a guide to immediate identification, note: hipped and gabled roofs are almost exclusively prewar or immediate postwar; steel windows are unusual after about 1955; double glazing or double windows are unusual before about 1965; 'Georgian' detail began to be fashionable about 1975; crosswall construction with very large windows dates from about 1958–70; central heating spread downwards through the market from about 1960 and was virtually universal in new houses by 1970.

What can you afford?

You may find that, although you have a good general idea of the sort of bracket your new home will come into, it is difficult to be precise because of the number of imponderables. You can't be sure what your present home, if you have one, will fetch or how much a building society will lend you, and house prices vary widely from one district to another.

It is generally considered that putting money into your own home is one of the best and safest investments, yet you need to keep at least some of your money free. The move itself, when everything is accounted for, will be expensive, and so on.

This chapter is intended to help you to work out how much you can afford to spend. Chapter 12 is concerned with the logistics of the actual financial transactions.

Your present assets

Unless you are a first-time purchaser, it is likely that your most important asset is your present home. You have probably, even if you borrowed heavily to buy it, paid off at least part of that loan, and the property may easily have appreciated in value as well. The problem is to decide just how much spare money you can expect to realise from the sale.

Firstly, study the market

The local paper will give a good guide to asking prices in your area, while further data can be collected from the displays in estate agents' windows. Notice, though, that the actual sale price may vary from the price at which the property is offered, that it may be higher or lower depending on the present state of the market – if sales are sticking, prices may be undercut to get a sale, whereas if there's competition to buy an 'auction' may develop, with the sale going to the highest offer – and that values can be widely different in adjacent districts or even streets.

Secondly, get a valuation

A professional surveyor, probably practising in the area as an estate agent, will be able to give a reasonably accurate price. He will tell you what asking price you should set, and whether to expect to come down or hope for an increase. If you ask him to sell for you, you probably won't have to pay for the valuation,

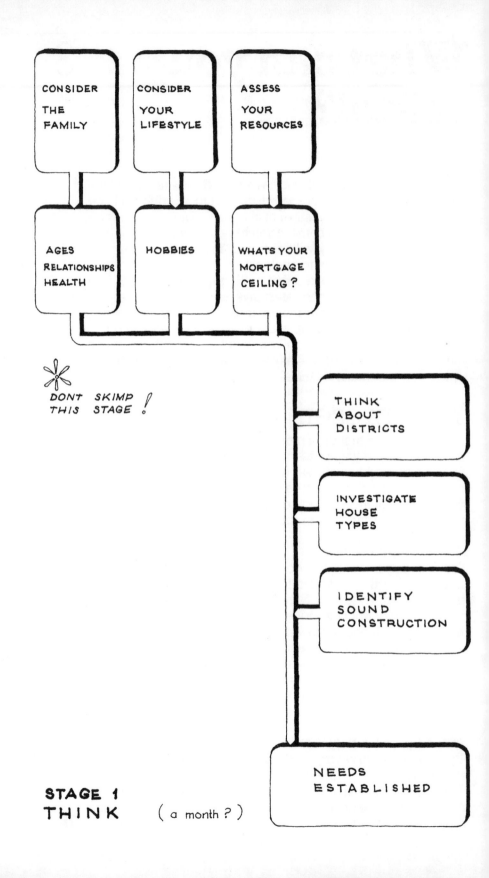

but otherwise he may charge something like 0·5 per cent of the value he puts on the house or flat.

Thirdly, offer the property for sale

If the building is in any way unusual, this may be unavoidable. You can sell subject to a specified delay in occupation. Some people put the property on the market without any intention of completing a deal, just to test the water. If you are asking too much you will get nibbles but few offers (and those on the low side) whereas if you name an unrealistically low figure you will have customers clamouring to buy.

There are two dangers in doing this: you might get such a good offer that you felt you couldn't pass it up, so leaving yourself with a time limit within which you must find a new place: you might put off buyers who see your house advertised again later, and wonder what went wrong the first time around. People who go to the trouble of viewing could feel justifiably annoyed. You may feel the tactic is rather unscrupulous.

You will have other assets as well. First-time buyers should add up the total of their realisable cash: savings accounts, premium bonds, stocks and shares may add up to an appreciable sum. The deposit they have accumulated in a building society account should be a major item.

Borrowing

Most people's principal asset besides their home is their ability to borrow. The great majority of house purchases are financed by borrowing money from one source or another, and the advantages and snags of these should be understood.

Building societies and bank mortgages

The main aim of building societies is to invest their savers' money in homes. They are, therefore, the first place where most potential borrowers enquire, and you should get as much literature as possible from as many of them as you can. Include some small local societies as well as some of the big national ones and the banks which have a considerable share of mortgage business.

You will find that there are two principal types of mortgage:

The 'repayment' mortgage

This is probably the most common. The monthly repayments are all equal, and each consists of an actual repayment component and some interest. At the beginning of the repayment period, the installments are largely interest (which attracts a tax concession), while towards the end a higher proportion of each payment goes towards paying off the actual loan.

The policy can be protected by a separate life insurance policy, which most borrowers think advisable. This means that the whole of the loan will be paid off by the insurance company if the borrower dies, so it is a helpful safeguard for a family.

The 'endowment' mortgage

This is closely linked to life insurance. An endowment insurance policy is taken out, which will pay off the loan in full at the end of the agreed period, and meanwhile the regular equal repayments consist almost entirely of interest on the loan, with a separate insurance premium on the borrower's life.

The life insurance in this case continues after the house is sold, and there is more tax relief than with a repayment mortgage, but the interest rate is usually higher. It's more beneficial to high than to low tax payers.

Within this context, there are other variations.

A 'with profits' mortgage is one which is more expensive but which provides you with a way of saving money, because you stand to gain extra money in the end, but it may not be the best investment for your savings.

Special mortgage schemes have been devised for a 'high start', so that a wife can contribute for a few years before the family limits her earning power, after which the payments are reduced.

There are also 'low start' schemes for families with good prospects, who expect promotions to improve their ability to pay. These seem a good idea for a great many people, because rises in earnings are generally relatively higher than rises in mortgage repayments.

In recent years interest rates generally have risen dramatically at times, and with them the level of mortgage repayments. Borrowers are often given the choice of *either*:

continuing the same level of repayment but extending the term of the mortgage (sometimes to the extent that the loan will never be paid off until the house is sold);

or

leaving the term unaltered but increasing the repayments, (sometimes to an unbudgeted high level).

When rates fall, a similar but opposite choice may also be offered. The choice is not available on all schemes or from all societies. Either of these methods of repayment is perfectly fair financially, but one or the other may be better suited to your financial position.

Building society investigations

Building societies naturally have a prime duty to their investors and are bound to be selective in the way they lay out their money. In addition, governments sometimes use the imposition of credit ceilings as a control on the national economy, so that there is temporarily actual rationing of mortgages. (This, incidentally, may mean that a society that is perfectly happy to lend to you has to delay for an appreciable period before doing so.)

In order to lend prudently, the societies have to make two kinds of important investigation, as follows.

The borrower

The first set of investigations concern the person who will be responsible for making the regular repayments. They need to be assured that he, she or they are not only capable of making these but sufficiently responsible to do so. To assess these points they will demand a considerable amount of personal information from you, as follows.

Name, address and relationships (if it's a joint mortgage).

How long you've been living at your present address, and if the period is short, where you lived previously.

Age and nationality.

Your credit and debt record, including any court judgements. If you can be proved to have a good record of paying off debts this will be in your favour. It's a fact of life that lenders are suspicious of anyone who's never been given credit before. If they use a credit reference agency to check your status, you are entitled to see the information on file.

What regular payments – maintenance, hire purchase, insurance – you are already committed to.

Your job, and whether you are paid by salary or by intermittent fees (as a freelance journalist or a barrister might be).

Your income from all other sources.

Your spouse's income, whether or not it's a joint mortgage.

The names of people like your employer or bank manager who will vouch for your probity. It's wise, as well as polite, to make sure in advance that such people are willing to speak for you.

Not every prospective borrower is regarded with equal favour by a lender. Groups who have reported difficulty include women, unmarried couples, people (like actors) with an irregular income, and, particularly, retired people. The last may have to protect any loan with a special insurance policy.

People who have demonstrated their ability to save regularly with a society often find that it stands them in good stead when they want a loan, and they are higher in the queue for a mortgage than non-savers. A savings account with a building society may be a good way of building up the money for a deposit for first-time buyers, and you need some strategic cash for the move anyway: it seems a diplomatic move to keep this in accounts at more than one building society.

The property

The second set of investigations is concerned with the property.

It is unusual for a society to decide *tout simple* that a prospective borrower is a good risk: its willingness to lend depends on the property, too. When you make your first tentative enquiries to a building society, it would be useful to have in mind one or two different types of home, so as to discover what the policy would be in each case.
Properties generally regarded as 'difficult' include:

- flats in converted buildings,
- houses without gardens,
- houses which lack basic facilities such as indoor sanitation (in which case a loan might be offered on condition that such amenities were provided),
- properties on short leases,
- buildings with 'unconventional' construction, such as a timber frame.

On the last point policy seems to have been somewhat liberalised recently.

Valuation

Apart from their general lending policy described below, a lender will not offer a loan until a specific property has been valued on his behalf. The borrower must pay the fee for this valuation (even if no loan is offered) and used never to know what the report contained, though nowadays he's likely to be able to see it. The valuation is *not* a structural survey, and though a recent court case appears to establish that a borrower can rely on it as evidence that the property is worth the price paid, it would be very dangerous to assume that you need have no separate structural survey done. See Chapter 6, p. 102.

Building society policy

At your first consultation, the society should be willing to tell you two things: one, the percentage of the purchase price they are willing to lend in normal circumstances on different types of property; and, two, your personal mortgage ceiling. This is based on your perceived ability to pay. It is likely to be expressed as a multiple of your salary (often twice or two-and-a-half times your salary), plus a rather lower multiple of a second (wife's?) salary.

Since not all societies operate on the same guidelines, either in their attitude to types of property or their assessment of people's reliability as repayers, it is worthwhile to investigate the policy of more than one, so as to find out where the terms that suit your circumstances best are to be found. You might find that a small local society is more flexible than one of the national giants.

If at any time you have a loan refused, ask whether it is you, the property or the economic situation which is at fault. When you enquire again, there or elsewhere, this will forearm you.

Other sources of finance

Insurance company

Insurance company mortgages are usually linked to life insurance and are very often of the 'endowment' type (see p. 78). Insurance companies don't usually give first mortgages, except perhaps to people who already have life insurance with them, but they may be prepared to offer 'top-up' mortgages.

This isn't very popular with building societies: their calculations have led to their estimate of the borrower's ability to pay, and they can't be expected to welcome him entering into a further very long-term commitment.

Bank loans (as opposed to mortgages, see above)

Bank loans are useful for short-term loans, such as bridging loans to see you over the actual changeover period. Borrowers pay the current overdraft rate of interest and may be eligible for tax relief on it if they make clear at the outset what the money is for. Bridging loans for an indefinite period should be avoided if at all possible.

Employers

If you are moving because your employer has redeployed you or to take up a new post, your employer may be willing to offer you a mortgage. The rates may be tempting – but there are strings attached: what would happen if you left the firm?

Private mortgage

Private individuals sometimes feel giving a mortgage is a good investment. Whether such a lender is your grandfather or a perfect stranger, any agreement for a loan should be properly entered into with well understood conditions on either side. The help of a solicitor in drawing up the documents is virtually indispensible.

Builder

If you think of buying a newly constructed house you may find that the builder offers you a mortgage. The rates may be advantageous because the firm has made a package arrangement with a building society. I would compare the deal with one that can be obtained elsewhere, but don't hesitate to enter into such an agreement if it suits your circumstances.

Sometimes the advantage is not so much financial but allows you to 'queue jump' in a time of mortgage famine.

Local authorities

Local authorities offer only repayment mortgages, and though they may be able to offer a high percentage of the total price, you might find the rate of interest high. The basis of calculation may differ from that used by a building society. Get details from the treasury at the town hall of the area you're moving to.

Mortgage brokers

Brokers with a wide-ranging experience of the various ways of raising money can be very helpful, especially if you have difficulty in finding a loan. There should be nothing for you to pay, unless a satisfactory loan is arranged (and usually not then). The broker is paid by the eventual lender.

Conditions of a loan

Wherever you borrow, there will be conditions attached. Make sure you see the standard conditions, and enquire about any special conditions that might affect the type of property you're interested in. Conditions could include that you undertake to:

- insert a damp-proof course,
- do major repairs,
- keep the property in good decorative order,
- insure it for a given sum, perhaps with one of three specified companies,
- inform the lender about any local authority plans you hear about which might affect the value,
- not let the building, or part of it, without permission,
- get the lender's approval to any alterations, whether or not you want to extend the mortgage to pay for them.

Cost of the move

Against your resources, you must set the total costs of the move. These will include the following:

- cost of obtaining a mortgage, including solicitor's fees and valuation,
- cost of your own survey (and possibly more than one, if you investigate more than one property),
- cost of selling your present home, including agent's fees, advertising, repairs, solicitor's fees,
- costs of househunting, including time off work, travelling expenses,
- cost of the conveyance (see Chapters 11 and 12),
- costs of the move, including removers' charges, renewal of carpets and curtains, travelling and possibly overnight accommodation,
- postal expenses.

Obviously there are many ways of minimising this expenditure, and later in the book I explain in particular the occasions on which professional help is essential and those on which you might be able to dispense with it. See Chapter 6 on surveys, Chapter 8 on expert help with remedial work and alterations, Chapter 11 on conveyancing, Chapter 13 on removals.

Life-cycle costs

If you were buying a car, you would be as much interested in running and maintenance costs as in the purchase price. A similar attitude when buying a home is prudent. This approach (it is known as 'terotechnology') is concerned with the total expenditure entailed by a purchase throughout its planned life, from which the resale or residual value of the property is deducted at the end of the period.

When choosing a home, you should evaluate not only the mortgage repayments but also:

• ground rent,
• rates,
• insurances on the property, its contents and yourself (not forgetting to take into account that insuring a car is dearer in some areas than others),
• repairs at a reasonable annual level,
• maintenance,
• service charges of flats,
• travel to and from work,
• any upgrading of your social life.

By doing this, you can work out whether an expensive place in town is actually dearer than a cheaper one in the country.

Summary

You now have a fairly clear idea of what you can afford, and are in a position to avoid getting ensnared by some delightful place that is really beyond your pocket.

Comparison of your dreams with what is on offer at your price may show you that you need to modify your ideas – usually, alas, by settling for more modest aspirations, though occasionally a family finds to its delight that it can actually fly a little higher than it imagined.

You are now ready to get yourself on to the books of agents, and to start househunting in earnest.

4 **Buying and selling**

You have now worked out your family's needs, and the priorities within them with some care; you have a general picture of the ways in which buildings satisfy such needs, and of the characteristics of houses and flats built at different times; you are clear about the amount of money you have to spend. Now is the time to enter the marketplace.

Buy first or sell first?

One of the most difficult decisions to make is whether to start with selling one's home *or* acquiring another. It's a difficult decision because market conditions at one time make one option safer and at others the other. Bear in mind the following points. The advantages of one are obviously the disadvantages of the other.

Advantages of buying first

You are sure of a home – you won't have to move into expensive rented accommodation or stay with friends because you have to leave one house before the other is ready.

You can take time to survey the market thoroughly and wait for the right property because you're not under pressure.

In a seller's market you can snap up a property directly you have the chance, without the risk of losing it to another buyer while you sell your present home: you are sure of being able to sell quickly.

Advantages of selling first

You know exactly how much money you can spend.

You don't risk having two mortgages at once, or an expensive bridging loan.

In a buyers' market, you can clinch a sale quickly, and be sure of finding a property to suit you quickly.

Using estate agents

When buying

The two major sources of information about property for sale are estate agents and local papers. It costs nothing to be on the books of a number of estate agents. The ones that carry the types of property in which you are interested should be easy to identify from their displays and advertisements.

Most firms mail a weekly list outlining the properties on their books – they may send the whole list to everyone, or they may send only the section in which the customer has expressed interest. After seeing the list you send for detailed particulars on any houses or flats you find interesting. This means a delay which, in a seller's market, can be fatal to your chances of getting the best property.

However, if you specify closely enough what you are looking for, many firms will send detailed particulars directly they have them. Many may seem quite unsuitable – outside the area you specified, the wrong number of rooms or wrong period – because they think you might on reflection find them worth considering.

They may advertise some houses before they have printed particulars to send out, so it's wise to look at the advertisements too, but don't rely on these entirely as they cover only a selection of available property in any one week. (Private sellers also advertise. There are usually no printed particulars, so you have to go to look at what's on offer, and it's less easy to write a property off on the basis of what you read.)

In general, if you've got details, try to weed out houses as ruthlessly as you can on the basis of the practical and financial criteria you've already established – otherwise you will make endless wasted journeys and become very weary of looking at quite unsuitable places.

One problem in doing this is that, until you have got used to it, the language used by estate agents is pretty remote from English as we know it. The key to understanding it is to appreciate that agents are in business to get the best possible price for the properties they are selling: their duty is to the vendor. If they can possibly praise a feature, they will do so. If they don't mention it then either it's absent or deficient. Most estate agents are perfectly honest in their descriptions – so look for the least appealing interpretation of each phrase! For example, any phrase implying that a room is less than grandiose ('cosy', 'compact') should be read as 'small'; if the description praises the proximity of some facility, it's reasonable to assume this causes some disturbance; 'secluded' may mean 'remote', and so on. At the end of the book (p. 201) you will find a glossary of estate agents' jargon.

You can rely on hearing of a large range of property from an agent, but you need not ignore places that are offered privately without the razzmatazz an agent might employ.

The agent may be helpful in getting a mortgage, but you need not feel constrained to go to the building society of which he is an agent. The buyer doesn't have to pay the agent. 85

When selling

The major skill of the agent lies in his close understanding of values and the working of the market, so that he can make a shrewd and reliable estimate of the right asking price for a property, as well as how much it is actually likely to realise. He can advise on the scale of advertisement appropriate, and is in a position to bring the qualities of a place on offer to the attention of a large number of potential buyers.

For this service he is paid a fee by the vendor. The fee varies from place to place and according to the details of the service offered, but you should expect to pay at least 1½ per cent of the purchase price. The fee may be reduced if you give the agent the 'sole rights', but that could mean that if you find a purchaser yourself you still have to pay the estate agent's fee. Some agents offer a 'no-sale-no-fee' service, and others charge a reduced fee, but charge extra for advertisements.

Selling without using an agent has attractions. It works in a sellers' market, and it is worthwhile in many circumstances trying to sell yourself for a week or two. You must be sure you are asking enough. If you get few nibbles and no offers after a couple of weeks, you probably need the expert.

If you think of selling yourself, remember:

- It is difficult to bring the property to the attention of buyers with little but an unillustrated advertisement and a sign in the window. Repeated advertising may be expensive.
- Considerable investigation is needed to establish the correct asking price, and how much to be prepared to come down when an offer is received. You could underprice by several times an agent's fee.
- You must be resident and available to show people round.
- You *must* use an agent if there is any question of selling at auction.

Doing your own selling

The following advice assumes that though you are not going through an estate agent you will, however, be using the services of a good solicitor – i.e. *this is not the start of do-it-yourself conveyancing.*

Apart from establishing the price (see Chapter 3) the vital stages in selling your own property are:

Composing the advertisement

Follow the experts in not drawing attention to weak points, but don't feel bound to use jargon. An honest description in clear English will do. Your best guide to knowing what to stress in writing this description is to consider what attracts you yourself to read a particular advertisement further.

Size and number of rooms are usually key points. Next might be the district and any special features of the siting. Age and sound construction should be mentioned. And be sure to include important selling points like central heating (mention if it's gas fired, but possibly don't mention the fuel otherwise), garage or garage space, cellar or loft that could be converted, and the type of garden (which will attract some buyers if it's small, others if it's large, so say which it is).

Preparing the house to be looked over
Try to make the family keep things reasonably tidy to give a good first impression. Take down lace curtains and keep windows sparkling, to look welcoming. Repair small but obvious faults. Get specialist reports on any cracks, damp or decayed wood. If you have time and money, get the remedial work done, and have the specification and guarantee ready to produce. Don't spend time and money on expensive redecoration.

Showing the house
Don't volunteer information, but be willing to answer questions. Don't draw attention to deficiencies, but don't let it look as if you're trying to conceal them, either. Check that the house doesn't smell of stale food, cats or anything else unpleasant. Fresh ground coffee covers many smells nicely. Learn from people's comments: they may give you a new perspective on what's good and bad about the house.

Auctions

Selling at auction
When you sell at auction you are bound to accept the highest bid *providing* it is higher than the 'reserve' you have put on the property. Deciding what the reserve should be is difficult, since properties are usually auctioned just because their value is difficult to fix: the advice of the auctioneer is invaluable, though you're not bound to take it. One way of arriving at a figure might be to consider how much prices have gone up since you bought, and vary the price you gave by that amount.

You will probably have to pay an auctioneer's fee even if the property is withdrawn because it didn't reach the reserve – and you would then be faced with finding some other way of selling it. Allow 1½% + VAT + cost of advertising.

In some cases, where the law imposes a duty to sell at the highest price, an auction sale is the only practicable method of testing the market.

After an auction is advertised, but before it occurs, the vendor may find that he is approached by various people 87 anxious to buy before the auction, to find out what the reserve is and to avoid the uncertainty of bidding. It is tempting to accept such an offer, but wiser to wait, however excruciating the delay may be. One sensible strategy is to agree to accept the offer if the property should be withdrawn because it fails to reach the reserve. Naturally you then ensure that the reserve is higher than the offer: the offer is treated as an early bid.

Since the successful bidder will be committed to buy, serious purchasers will wish to have surveys made before the date of the auction and you may find this inconvenient. A way round is to commission a full structural survey yourself which you then, with the consent of the surveyor, make available to any serious enquirer.

The most important aspect of an auction, apart from establishing the real market value, is that there is no going back on either side once a bid has been accepted. Everyone who expects to bid has to get their solicitor to make the necessary investigations in advance so that they have excluded any major problems and are ready to enter into a binding contract.

Buying at auction

If you are considering buying at an auction *read the passage above*, and bear in mind that because you will be committed if your bid is accepted you must first have:

- checked out any legal aspects, preferably using a solicitor,
- got a survey,
- obtained the offer of a mortgage.

There is nothing to stop you from making an offer in advance of the auction, but don't expect it to be accepted with alacrity.

Selling a house with faults

It may be that, whether you're selling yourself or using an agent, prospective buyers keep withdrawing because they have difficulty in getting a mortgage. This may be because the building society has found some fault with your property – a crack, damp, or something of the kind.

There are two ways of getting over this problem:

- Get a specialist report, put matters right, and be ready to show the report, specification and guarantee to enquirers, especially surveyors valuing the property.
- Undertake to pay for repairs and remedial work done under the supervision of the purchaser's surveyor.

If you feel sure the problem is less serious than it appears at first sight, it might be worth commissioning a structural survey of your own to prove the point. If it does so, there should be no difficulty in anyone getting a mortgage from the society for whom your surveyor reports. Indeed, you might be able to make a selling point of the fact that you knew where a mortgage could be had.

Council tenants

The sale of council houses to sitting tenants is really outside the scope of this book because it does not involve househunting. If you are thinking of buying one, I would suggest you weigh up very carefully the advantages and disadvantages:

- It should be cheaper, because of the discounts allowed for the fact of your occupation and how long you have been there.
- You won't have to move in order to own your own home.
- You can retain the improvements you have made.
- You are more likely to be able to do what you like to your home without permission than if you still rent it.
- You will eventually have a realisable asset.
  But,
- Social factors may impose a ceiling on the price you can sell for.
- You can't sell straightaway without foregoing the discount you got when buying.

The decision will be a delicate balance of social and financial factors on which it would be difficult for anyone who doesn't know you, the house and the area to advise you. However, for most people, because of the potential tax-free capital gain, the decision will be as to whether or not they are prepared to commit themselves to stay in the house for five years from the date of purchase.

For further guidance on buying and selling, see Chapter 11 (legal) and Chapter 12 (financial).

5 How to view

Most people's first impressions of a newly encountered property are highly subjective. They notice the roses round the door or the mess in the hall and this colours everything they observe. It's essential to be alert for this and allow for it.

Which properties will you view?

You will be sent a mass of sets of particulars by the various agents whose lists you are on, and will also see advertisements that seem tempting. You couldn't possibly visit them all, but you need some way of ensuring that you *do* view every property that might suit you.

Read *all* the particulars that are sent to you with care: if nothing else they will help to sharpen your perception of values in that particular place at that particular time. This is especially important if you are moving into or out of London. Prices in the capital are so much higher than elsewhere that it generally takes someone coming to town or moving to the provinces some time to get the hang of them.

In order to decide which flats or houses to actually visit you need to have a realistic idea of where you're prepared to compromise on what you want, and where your heels will remain firmly dug in. You might use a scoring system to clear your minds on this. Make a list of the ten aspects of a home which are most important to you, placing them in order of importance. Award a high score for features that are vital to you and a lower one for things you consider desirable but not essential. When you make your first visit to any house give it marks from one to five for each aspect. Total the score to find out the best property which is nearest to your ideal.

The main thing is to look at all factors and not just ones that strike you at a first reading.

Making sketch plans

Because you are anxious not to miss a good buy you may find yourselves considering a large number of potential homes, and however rigorously you select you may still find yourselves visiting three or more places on the same Saturday morning. Unless you keep careful notes you will never remember again which house it was that had the pretty fireplace and which the awkward cellar stairs.

This is why I suggest you seriously consider teaching yourself to make rapid notes in the form of sketch plans. You may think this quite out of the question for you, and much prefer to talk into a cassette recorder or keep notes in some other form as you go round. However, for those who want to take the plunge, I'm now going to describe a simple way of making a useful plan. (Try this out on your present home and those of your friends. You will find it adds little to the time taken to look round a property – and I promise that the skill isn't difficult to acquire.)

First of all, stand in the hall with your back to the front door and try to draw the shape of the hall floor. All the doors are probably about the same width, which should help, and you may find working on squared paper gives you a good guide. To get the length of the wall between doorways right, try to estimate how many door widths would go into the space. Put in the foot of the stairs.

Now go into one of the rooms and add the plan of that to your drawing, then into another and so on until the whole ground

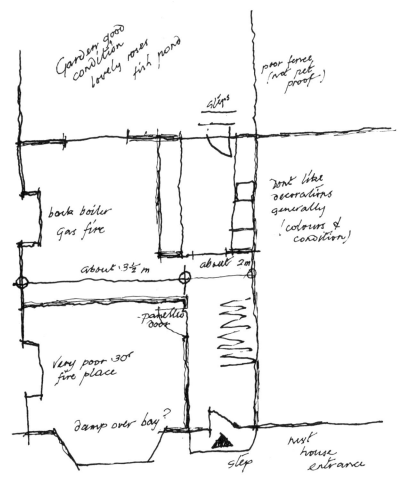

floor is down on paper. The doorways give you the connection between one room and another. Go outside and see whether you have got any odd corners and recesses you can't account for: this is easily done when you are estimating sizes.

When you are pretty sure the ground-floor plan is accurate, you can use it as a basis for plans of the other floors: outside walls usually coincide.

With a little practice, you will find that you can make quite a respectable record (it's for your own use, so it doesn't need to look professional, of course). It makes a very good basis for noting down particular features you want to remember about the house.

I don't feel you need be shy of making these sketches, but I know some people feel they don't want to seem quite that interested! If that's how you feel, stop the car round the corner and try to make plans there, *before* you go on to look at the next house on your list. This will fix the layout in your mind, and will be a useful reminder when you try to remember and compare places at home later.

Your main reason for making this visit is to decide whether the property is worth a detailed check. Don't look for detail. You are mainly there to assure yourselves that the particulars are accurate, and that there are no obvious serious faults: detail will come later.

Look particularly at

Number of rooms
Are there really all the rooms promised, or has someone optimistically designated a glory hole as a bedroom, or an outside store as a utility room?

Size and shape of rooms
Are there any rooms that are so long and narrow that they would be difficult to furnish? Are all the rooms described as 'double bedrooms' actually big enough? (10–11 sq m, 110–20 sq ft).

Windows
Make a rough note of the size and type of windows, and whether they get morning or afternoon sun. Are any of them overlooked (or would they be if the trees were bare)? If 'double glazing' is claimed, is it 'real' double glazing, or secondary windows? Note the view.

Storage
Make a note on your drawing of all built-in storage. Check that wardrobes that look built-in actually are.

Services
Make sure you know which services are available as well as which are actually installed.

Condition
Make brief notes of which rooms need decorating, and any repairs that are obviously needed.

Garden
Check the size and the state of the garden and fences. Does it get enough sun?

Neighbours
Be sure you know what is on the other side of the fence – it could be a glue factory!

In virtually any house there will be features that strike you as particularly attractive, or particularly unsympathetic. It takes a deliberate effort not to let such points outweigh your objective observations – and you could later regret abandoning a promising prospect because the tiles in the bathroom were the wrong colour, or buying a place that was thoroughly inconvenient but had a pretty view.

On no account express too much interest in the property at this stage, or give the impression that you are a sure buyer. If, when you've had time to add up your impressions and talk it over, you think you may be seriously interested, make an appointment to come back and look round thoroughly, when you can devote more time to it. Be sure that the vendor knows you mean to spend time and care on this later inspection: he ought not to mind because it shows you're really interested. Chapter 6 describes this later visit.

The district

To most people, living in the right area is as important as having a convenient home. Indeed, I would say that the most important factor to take into account when deciding which properties to view is the neighbourhood.

Districts are rarely static: they are either gently falling into decay or steadily improving their status, and it can be very difficult for a visitor to see which is happening. It is, however, important if you are intending to put down roots. It is obviously highly advantageous to identify an area on the point of going up in the world – where a property is likely to appreciate in value. To be a pioneer entrant into such an area means being part of a new, growing and vigorous community and having a share in setting its tone. It may entail some of the discomforts of the pioneer in the early months, of course, but can be very rewarding.

Many families are relúctant to look for a home in a 'twilight' area because of the risk that the area might go down rather than up. But you will find the signs if you know what to look for.

Area going up

Signs of a district that's improving – which is happening in an increasing number of once-abandoned inner-city suburbs – include the following.

A flourishing community group actively working to stop undesirable developments as well as keeping a range of social activities going. Try to get hold of the newsletter of any such group, which will give you a clear idea not only of its theoretical objectives but also of its actual operation. Talk to the Secretary if you can. Activities you might appreciate could include a 'welcome wagon', playgroup, dramatic and choral societies. Look out for any sign of 'do-goodery' which would imply that one section of the community takes a rather patronising attitude to another. A good community group ought also to be keeping the community as a whole informed about intentions of the local authority and others involved in the area, but not necessarily opposing each and every pro-posal for change. No doubt if they are vigorous they will know how to mobilise local opinion when this appears desirable.

Churches that are clearly flourishing, and have buildings and grounds that are well looked after. Even if you are not yourselves particularly interested in church activities, you will find that they are a good barometer of the health of a community, and a glance at the notice boards and parish magazine will give you a picture of the life of the district.

A variety of shops, especially specialist food shops. Those that sell ethnic foods, health foods or other goods of interest to particular communities are naturally likely to be found where their customers live, so you will get a good impression of a community by looking at its shops. Sainsbury's and Mothercare tell you, just as much as Patel's Oriental Grocery or the Wholefood Cooperative, who lives in the area.

Well-maintained houses and cared-for gardens indicate a pride in personal property that residents are likely to extend to concern for their neighbourhood. Beware, however. The response of some home owners to a suspicion that their district may be deteriorating is a fierce determination to keep their own part up properly.

Many of the most sought-after areas have a variety of sizes, types and prices of homes, so that there is a genuine mixed community like that of a village.

Danger signs: area going down

While many older residential areas are proudly and carefully kept attractive by their residents, there are others that are going inexorably downhill. This may be because there is something in their environment, such as a motorway or a polluting factory, which makes it impossible to rescue the area, or because the houses have, over the years, been allowed to get beyond economic repair. The househunter new to a district can find it hard to discover which areas these are, but can look for clues.

Cheap house prices compared to a neighbouring district means that houses are hard to sell: this implies an unpopular and therefore deteriorating area. It can be salutary to price houses of kinds other than that in which you are actually interested. You may discover that there is a price ceiling above which houses can't be sold, so that larger properties go into multiple or office use. This would mean that a householder who buys a run-down property and does it up will be unlikely to get his money back.

Any property which has been on the market for a longer period than the average at that time is a danger sign, especially if there seems to be a large number of properties on the market in the area. (Of course this varies over the years – in a buyers' market it may be many months, while in a sellers' it is a week or two.) There may be many reasons for the failure to sell, but one could be that locals in the know regard the area as one to avoid.

Patchy demolition may mean that there is a comprehensive redevelopment scheme in the wind. Visit the local planning office at the town hall and ask to see the area or district planning officer or one of her assistants. (You may have to make an appointment, but don't be palmed off with the person at the enquiry desk.) She will be able to tell you what developments are under consideration for the area, and should show you the district plan. This will tell you which shopping areas are scheduled for improvement, what limits the local authority puts on multiple occupancy (houses being split up into flats or bedsitters), and so on. You should be alerted to any new urban motorway proposals or a compulsory purchase order that's imminent (with the 'planning blight' that could ensue).

Ill-maintained houses and untended gardens are a danger sign: they often indicate rented property, which is commonest in less attractive areas.

Empty houses that have been allowed to become derelict are probably unsaleable for a reason: the reason could apply to other property in the vicinity. Perhaps differential settlement or planning blight or a property too large for a modern family but too small for institutional use could be the cause.

Multiple occupancy of largish houses that would make good family homes indicates that the families who could afford to live in them prefer to live elsewhere. This isn't damning: the tide towards multiple occupancy has in many places been turned, and many such houses are well maintained.

Shops poorly stocked with flyblown window displays.

Many houses converted to commercial or professional use.

Look at churches, pubs and schools. Standards the community tolerates in its public buildings are a good guide to its view of itself.

If you have trouble getting a mortgage, ask whether it has anything to do with the district. Perhaps the building society feels that even property in good condition in that area is a poor investment.

Finding out more about the district

Most property advertisements are uninformative as far as areas are concerned, relying on charismatic names (that might sometimes stretch the boundaries recognised by the post office) and vague suggestions of popularity or proximity to excellent facilities.

A district should be examined as carefully as a home. Indeed, it may be wise provisionally to identify one or two general districts you like before even looking at individual properties. The one feature of a residence that's quite unchangeable is its siting. It's usually necessary to make a number of visits under quite different circumstances: if you do all your househunting on Sunday afternoons you may never know about the rowdy fish and chip shop, the lack of a good butcher or even the insistent bells that wake everyone at 7 am on Sundays.

Besides visiting and looking, it's highly desirable to chat to people. Find out whether general attitudes seem likely to be compatible with your own, how mixed the community is, whether residents are proud of their district and of belonging to it. You hope, of course, that such pride wouldn't mean hostility to newcomers. Take some points with a grain of salt – home ground may not be run down to outsiders.

If there is an opportunity, talking to other incomers can be revealing: the vicar, the doctor, the teachers at the school may come into this category. If you're moving to a new job, your new colleagues will probably help. If you notice any tendency to be surprised that you have chosen the area, think twice – you mightn't be happy.

Specific points to investigate include the following.

Rates

Rateable value isn't very informative unless you know the rate in the pound that's levied. Ask at the finance department of the town hall or at the local library. Make sure that you know whether the water rate is levied separately.

Shops

Most people ideally would like a small shopping centre within ten minutes' walk, with more than one grocer (for competition), a good butcher, baker, greengrocer and so on – and a major complex, maybe an hour away, where they would find Woolworths, Boots and other department stores. It's not only inconvenient to have less facilities than this, it can be expensive, too. This isn't because a sole village grocer exploits his position but because overheads are genuinely higher.

Try actually shopping in the locality, and compare prices with those you're used to paying for a whole shopping basket. Look for a good variety of brands and the particular items (ground coffee, cheeses?) that matter to you.

Schools

Whether you have school-aged children or not, you should investigate the local schools, first through the local education authority and secondly by talking to parents. If you are a parent yourself, the head teacher of the local school should welcome a visit by appointment. You need to know where the schools are (not least because you probably don't want to live next door to a noisy playground). A school on the same side of the main road as your house can save years of escort duty.

Find out, if you can, whether the local children actually go to the nearest school, and if not why not. It could be an oddity of boundary drawing, or the special popularity of a rival establishment. In the latter case *your* kids would probably have to go to the nearest school because that's the one with most vacancies. Parents sometimes choose a district purely on the basis of the catchment area for a particular school. This can put house prices on one side of a road higher than those opposite – a point worth bearing in mind if you don't have children.

Entertainments and leisure facilities

In the light of your own leisure interests you'll know whether you're more likely to be keen on a golf course or a dog track in the vicinity. In either case (and of course in the case of any other leisure facilities) you will probably not want this to be *too* close by; golf balls through the greenhouse, or the noise of a crowd, can be wearing if too often repeated.

Playing fields next door are a particular nuisance: people are always coming for their ball back, and not always asking first.

Other facilities

It is wise to check that doctors, dentists, clinics, churches, pubs and other facilities are not only present but welcoming. The doctor with the nicest waiting room and the best appointment system may have a full list.

Transport

Even if you expect to go everywhere by car, check the public transport services for the sake of visitors, your children and the lady who helps with the cleaning. It is not only important to have a reasonably frequent service, it also matters that at rush hour every bus isn't full before it gets to your stop. Look at the routes as well: you may want a cross-town service (to a hospital or friend's house) as well as one into town.

The local transport authority probably publishes timetables and a route map. In London, underground details are easy to get – try St James's Park underground station if you can't get the information elsewhere.

Parking

If there is no car park provided at the local shopping centre find out where cars park. This may be important in two ways: it may involve humping shopping a long way, and the road you are considering living in may be exactly where everyone parks, making access for you and your visitors very difficult.

If there is a popular pub, the same may apply in the evenings.

Find out by inspection, looking at yellow lines in the road, and decide where you would park when visiting any of the popular establishments in the area. Remember that wedding cars from the parish church or registrar's office can be just as much of a nuisance as any others, and might occur every Saturday through the summer. Funerals don't often park in the road.

Rat runs

The main access roads round some of our cities are so clogged with cars morning and evening that the more enterprising motorists explore residential roads to find ways of avoiding the bottlenecks. The 'rat runs' they create can bring a stream of speeding cars through otherwise quiet neighbourhoods twice a day, with considerable nuisance and some danger. The only way to discover whether a particular road is part of such a route is to be there at rush hour to see for yourself.

Pollution

Air and water may seem healthy but be polluted by effluents: some coastal authorities still discharge untreated sewage into the sea. Farm effluents may pollute streams and farms are often noisy. Industrial smoke and effluents also cause contamination to air and water and the plant may be unbelievably noisy.

Places of entertainment are often noisy, and so are their patrons when leaving.

The best source of information, besides observation, on all types of pollution, is the environmental health officer at the town hall, who will be able to provide details of any special hazards (as well as help in fighting them). As he spends a great deal of time around his patch, it's best to write rather than call.

Coastal erosion

Beware of any area with crumbling cliffs. This is a matter for very careful enquiry and insurance may be difficult to get (as well as expensive) if there is any danger of erosion. Ask for the chief engineer at the town hall (you'll probably get an assistant), and employ a local surveyor to look at any property, asking him to report specifically on this point.

Airfields

It isn't only commercial airfields that create a nuisance. RAF and USAF can do so too. Small and undeveloped fields may be developed later into far more active undertakings, and though protests from affected residents are inevitable, they're time and money consuming and not always effective. (They do a splendid job of inculcating community spirit, of course.) Find out about airfields from the 1:50 000 Ordnance Survey map – your first investment when considering an area.

Motorways

Be sure that you know not only what motorways exist, but whether any are projected, too. The amount of traffic on 'main' roads can be multiplied if the highway becomes a feeder to a motorway. (Ask the town hall planning department.)

Weather

An area which is idyllic in summer can be cut off by snow or by torrential rain in the winter. Another district which is delightful in spring and autumn might be intolerably exposed to hot summer sun or winter gales. Since it's impractical to wait to find out, some exercise of the imagination may be obligatory to explore such possibilities. Try to visualise snow built up in the narrow lane, the gentle hill stream in flood and so on.

Tourists

The district which attracts you may very easily attract holidaymakers too. It may seem a rather less desirable place when the holiday season is at its height than when you visit it early in the year. Parking may be difficult and expensive, there may be picnickers or caravans in the field next door and a great deal of litter. You may, of course, be prepared to put up with all this as the price for the undoubted privilege of living in such a delightful spot for the remainder of the year.

Alternatively, some ex-tourist purchasers are enchanted by an area in which they have spent happy holidays, and when the opportunity offers determine to buy a home there. They need to be aware that the district will change subtly out of season. Apart from the closure of many of the facilities (the theatre, perhaps, and some shops), the bracing breeze may be a howling gale in February and the winter mists may obscure the view for much of the year.

Boundaries
A county or district boundary running through what seems to be a coherent community can cause problems. These won't be insuperable, but do look into them. If you happen to live on the 'wrong' side of the road it could mean, for example, that you have to be on the list of a doctor in a distant area, would be sent to a hospital several miles away, and would have to wait for an ambulance to come a long way in an emergency. Libraries, schools and so on might be affected, too. Ask at the library, CAB or health centre, and take such points into account along with other features.

Local newspaper
An economical way to get the 'feel' of any district you consider moving to is to take the local newspaper for a few weeks. This will give a good idea of the local activities and controversies as well as a guide to house prices in the area. You can arrange this through your own newsagent.

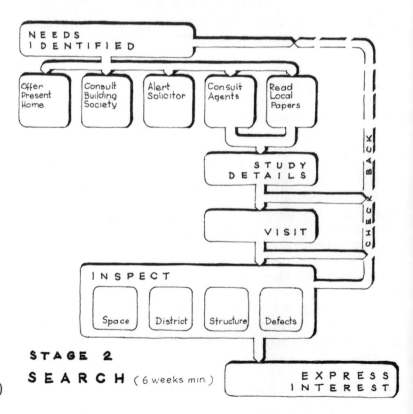

STAGE 2

SEARCH (6 weeks min.)

The weight given to all the different factors I have mentioned in connection with the district will be different in every case, of course, just as priorities vary over the home itself. What matters to people buying a retirement home may be level roads and good public transport; someone buying for investment may feel a 'good' address is vital. A group of friends buying cooperatively will probably want to be near to all their jobs and entertainment, while a family with small children will be looking for safe parks.

I can't, thank goodness, tell anyone at all what kind of district they would enjoy living in. We all very properly have our own preferences. What I want to emphasise is the importance of choosing the neighbourhood with as much care as you choose the flat or house. The most splendid residence won't make up for living in the wrong place.

6 **Your detailed inspection**

This chapter describes a method you could adopt when you go back to look in detail at a property that seems promising, what you should look for and the way you can most easily record what you see. Chapter 7 deals with the interpretation of what you see.

A professional survey

A complete examination and report from a qualified surveyor is of course needed for any building you seriously intend to buy. He should be a member of the Royal Institution of Chartered Surveyors, the Incorporated Society of Valuers and Auctioneers, or the Incorporated Association of Architects and Surveyors, and will have the skill and equipment to make an exhaustive investigation as well as the experience and knowledge to interpret his observations. As well as reporting on the present state of the property he will make recommendations about any work which may be needed. Chapter 8, p. 150 goes into detail on how to find and make the best use of a professional adviser like a surveyor, and you should take care to read that.

So, though your own careful examination can tell you whether or not it is worthwhile commissioning a full structural survey, you would be *very unwise* to rely entirely on your own inspection, except in the case of very recently completed buildings (such as those still covered by the National House Building Council guarantee).

Be careful, too, to distinguish between the valuation made on behalf of the building society (which is to satisfy the lender that he would get his money back if you reneged on the payments) and a structural survey which alerts *you* to potential and actual defects.

Fees for a survey are based on the amount of time taken to travel to the house, inspect it and prepare a report. You may be able to save something by asking for a report which only highlights problems: the survey will still be as comprehensive, since the surveyor is implying that anything not mentioned in his report is satisfactory.

It is wise to use a local surveyor, not only to save on the cost of travelling time but because local knowledge is invaluable in picking up the cause of faults. The local man will know the tricks of construction used in the area, as well as the geographical conditions.

Your inspection

Before you begin your inspection, I suggest you skim this whole chapter. It may seem dauntingly complicated, but that is because I have tried to make it as comprehensive as possible. No-one will need to look at *every* point, but you need to check through to decide in advance which points are relevant to the particular house or flat. Then I hope you will find you can use the chapter as a reference while you are actually making your inspection, and that it will help to ensure that you don't miss something vital.

To help you find your way through the mass of material, here are the pages on which you will find various important topics:

Don't be put off if this all seems very elaborate: I've had to cover points that would be relevant for families with young children as well as those important to the elderly; notes about flats as well as those about houses, and so on. You will also find that working systematically helps you to keep a clear picture of each place you look at, and is actually easier in the long run.

Equipment

You ought to be properly equipped, and I suggest you should take along, as well as an open mind (you may have been impressed by a single point, but you've got to take a cool look at everything!), someone else to cross check with, a clipboard, various felt-tip pens, a screw driver, a short steel tape, your sketches. A mirror, a ball, a torch and a pair of field glasses would also be invaluable, and you might take a camera. Take a note of the sizes of your major pieces of furniture.

The point about drawings is that it's quicker to record things on sketches than in notes, and be sure they're right. They don't have to be very professional: only you are going to use them.

Explain to the vendor that you are likely to be quite a long time on the job, and get his permission before you disturb anything. Politely decline his offer of help.

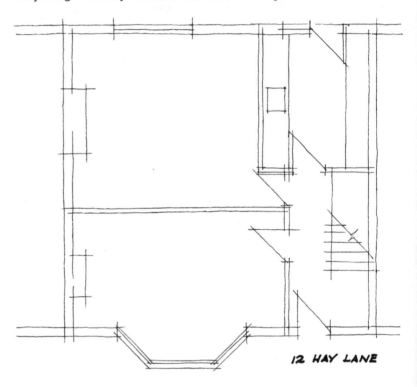

12 HAY LANE

Method

I suggest you start on the top floor or in the loft, and work clockwise around each room, floor by floor till you reach the cellar. Next go outside and work round the house looking at each wall from roof down to the ground. Finally, inspect paths, drains, hedges and garden before having a general look at the
district and nearby buildings.

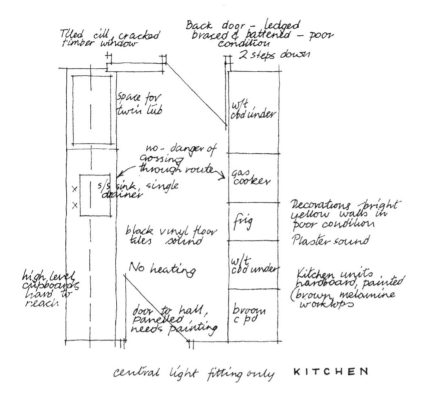

Tiled cill, cracked timber window

Back door - ledged braced & battened - poor condition
2 steps down

Space for twin tub

w/t cbd under

no - danger of crossing through route

gas cooker

s/s sink, single drainer

Decorations bright yellow walls in poor condition

Plaster sound

frig

black vinyl floor tiles sound

No heating

w/t cbd under

Kitchen units hardboard, painted (brown melamine worktops)

high level cupboards hard to reach

door to hall, panelled, needs painting

broom cpd

central light fitting only   **KITCHEN**

Whatever you look at, you need to note what it's made of, how big it is, its position and its condition. At this stage, don't try to *diagnose* any defects: you are recording enough information to let you go away and do this, at least provisionally, later. Chapter 7 will help the process.

Don't expect perfection, every property has faults.

Interior

In each room, ask yourself the following questions.

Walls

Is it solid or hollow? Tell by tapping it.

Does it carry the floor or roof above? You'll need to check the direction of floor boards, which run *parallel* to the wall carrying the floor.

Is it straight and upright? Leaning or bulging might be important, so estimate how far out of line the wall is.

Are there any cracks? If there are, make careful notes. You'll need to look at the whole pattern of cracking in the building to work out what's the cause. The width of the crack may be as important as its position, so estimate this (see which coin fits in, for example) and in particular note which part of the crack is 105

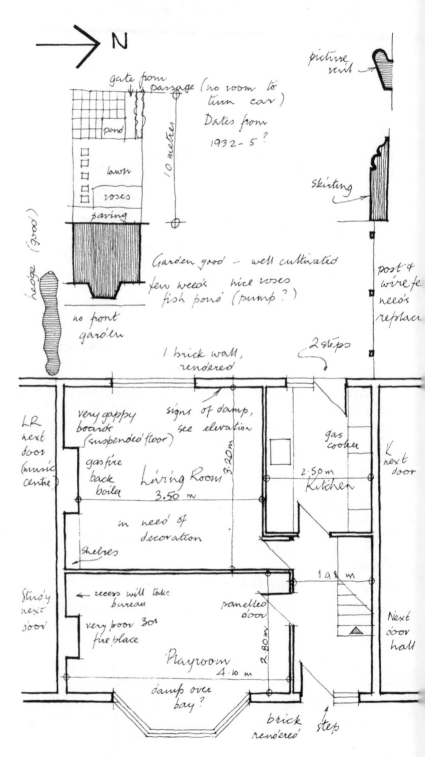

N →

picture rail

gate from passage (no room to turn car) Dates from 1932-5?

pond

skirting

10 metres

lawn
roses
paving

hedge (good)

Garden good - well cultivated
few weeds   nice roses
fish pond (pump?)

no front garden

post & wire fe
needs replac

2 steps

1 brick wall, rendered

signs of damp, see elevation

LR next door (music centre)

very gappy boards (suspended floor)

gas fire back boiler

gas cooker

K next door

Living Room
3.50 m

3.20m

2.50 m

Kitchen

in need of decoration

shelves

Study next door

← recess will take bureau

very poor 30s fire place

panelled door

1.98 m

2.80m

Next door hall

Playroom
4.10 m

damp over bay?

brick rendered

step

106

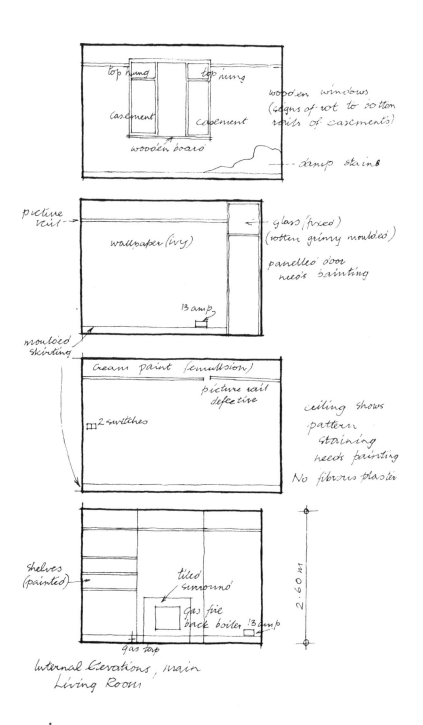

top hung top hung

casement casement

wooden board

wooden windows
(signs of rot to bottom
rails of casements)

— damp stains

picture rail →

wallpaper (ivy)

← glass (fixed)
(rotten grimy moulded)

panelled door
needs painting

13 amp

moulded
skirting

Cream paint (emulsion)

picture rail
defective

2 switches

ceiling shows
pattern
staining
needs painting
No fibrous plaster

shelves
(painted) →

tiled
surround

gas fire
back boiler 13 amp

2.60 m

gas tap

Internal Elevations, main
Living Room

widest. Note, too, whether the wall on one side of the crack is in front of that on the other. This can all helpfully be noted on an exaggerated sketch.

Is there any sign of damp? Look for discoloured or bleached wall paper, paper loose from the wall, powdery plaster or loose tiles. Note the position: here again it will be your notes from the whole property that help you decide where the water might be coming from. See also Chapter 7, p. 140.

Does the wall feel warm or cold? Chapter 7, p. 146, explains why this may matter.

Is the covering in good condition? Look at tiles to see that they aren't cracked or loose. Note the colour.

Does the plaster show any faults? If it's powdery, or loose from the wall (tell by tapping), try to note how widespread the trouble is. A variety of other faults (shininess, irregularity and so on) can be fairly easily corrected when decorating, but are worth noting.

Is the paintwork sound? Defects here generally result from poor preparation before painting, or from painting over damp. Any paintwork which is blistered or peeling will have to be got off before redecoration, so note it.

Do you like the decorations? You don't have to live with decorations you hate, but replacing them costs money.

Is there a skirting board? What is it like? Older, elaborate skirtings are expensive to match if repairs are needed.

Is the board in good condition? Look for irregular grain, which might be a clue to decay, and for loose or missing knots. A prod with your screwdriver may show the wood is unsound. If it is, look with special care at all other timbers.

Doors

Are the door frames sound? Check as above. The frame may be metal or wood, and the 'stop' may be part of it or 'planted' on. There's usually a strip called the architrave which neatens the edge of the plaster. The weight of the door is carried on the frame itself. If the frame is metal look for bubbling which means rust. Swing the door to see if it sags or binds. Check the hinges (there should be three on heavy doors, and they should be brass if the door is hardwood). Note that some hinges automatically close the door, and lift the door clear of a carpet square (though not of a fitted carpet).

Is the door panelled or flush? Be suspicious of doors which have been covered to look flush, but are really panelled underneath. They are specially liable to warp.

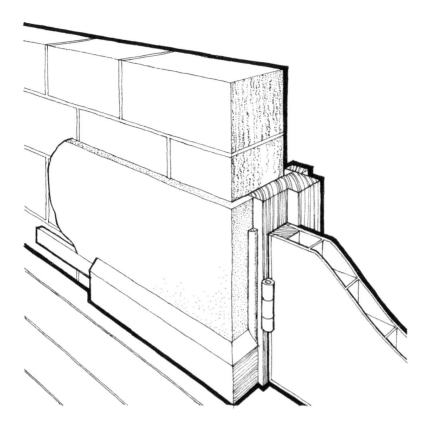

Are the handles and so on appropriate and in good condition? Make sure bolts and latches close properly.

Windows

Are the windows wood, steel, aluminium or some other material? If wood, look specially for blackish, soft wood along bottom rails, and for well-maintained paintwork. If steel, look hard for any sign of rust. Aluminium doesn't need to be painted.

How does the window open? You need to be sure that all the parts that are meant to open actually do (or that it doesn't matter). Note that an area of window equal to one-twentieth of the area of the floor should open, for adequate ventilation. You may want more than that for ease of cleaning, or to open up the house to the garden.

Check the fittings. Do they work? Are there burglar latches? Check sash cords for fraying.

What sort of curtain track/pelmet/blind is there? Will they leave it?

Check the state of decorations.

Is there double glazing? Recognise this by looking at the edges of panes for the double thickness, or for double reflections.

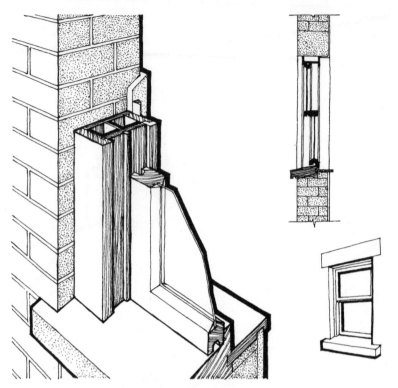

Worry if there are signs of damp between the panes – they're poorly sealed.

Are there double windows? Are they removable? Does the arrangement of panes in them match that of the windows? Can you get at both sides of both panes to clean them?

Electricity

Where are the socket outlets and electric switches? Look for square-pin, thirteen-amp sockets, preferably switched rather than any other type. They are a clue to modern wiring, but you will check this elsewhere. *If you see adaptors or trailing flexes in use, either of which is a hazard, this is a sign that the electric installation is inadequate.* Switches should be flush with the plaster, and plastic is safest.

Gas

Are there any gas points? If there are you could put in a gas fire, but beware of taps sticking up to be tripped over or even inadvertently turned on.

Is there a smell of gas? If there is, go and tell the owner straight away.

Are there any flues, including ones to boilers or gas appliances? If there is a blocked fireplace, is there a ventilator (the flue should have an air current maintained)?

Water

Mark every pipe, bothering less about what it does than where it is. Measure the distance from floor or ceiling at both ends, and check whether it's hot or cold. Look at the joints. Modern pipework has screw or sleeve fittings, 'wiped' joints that just look like a thickening of the pipe indicate lead pipes. Lead may be worth recovering – and lead water pipes *should* be removed as lead is a cumulative poison and slightly soluble in water.

Look for taps and drainage points on the pipes. Stop taps have recognisable 'tap' heads but no outlet, while drainage points are at the bottom of the run and have both.

What type of traps have sanitary fittings got? Every connection has a bend in the pipework to hold water and protect against drain smells. This may be part of the appliance (as in a WC), or a removable 'bottle' trap which is convenient to clean (as under a sink, for example), or it may have an unscrewable cap at the bottom for access, or it may be inaccessible. The last can be hard to clear if they get blocked.

What is the material of the sanitary fittings? Note especially enamel, which may chip or craze, wear thin with age, or stain badly. If it's stained the fitting may need to be replaced. Also note stainless steel, which is durable and easy to look after, and glass-reinforced plastic or acrylic, which are now much used for baths and slightly flexible. This means the seal between the bath and the wall is difficult to keep watertight. Get permission to remove bath panels, to check for signs of damp or rot: rot under baths is a serious problem.

Is there a drain smell? If so, try running water *gently* down the outlet, to see if that helps. If it doesn't, make a note to pay particular attention to drains, later.

Ceiling

Is the ceiling plastered, or made from some other material, such as wooden slats or plastic tiles? If there are expanded polystyrene tiles, try to find out how old they are as older ones may be a fire hazard.

Is there any sign of 'pattern staining'? If you can see dark marks between the joists, making stripes across the ceiling, this is often a sign of poor insulation in a loft above.

Are there any cracks? If so, plot them carefully as you did before, but they're rather less likely to be significant than those to walls. (See also p. 129.)

Does the ceiling sag? This could be caused by water or snow lying above, because the roof is faulty, or, more seriously, by 111 decay of supporting timbers. It always demands further investigation, and if it's noticed on a lower floor would make it very important to get a look at the floor above, even if this meant lifting a fitted carpet.

Is there decorative fibrous plasterwork? The cornices, central roses and so on which are often a feature of older ceilings are heavy. They may be difficult to match if they need repair.

Where are the lighting and switch points? (See also walls, p. 105.) The arrangement of furniture may be seriously affected by this. The drops to ceiling light fittings should be modern sheathed cable and not old-fashioned twisted flex, especially if that is fabric covered. The latter is a sign of an obsolete wiring system.

Are the ceiling roses, from which the drops hang, modern and in good condition?

How is the ceiling decorated?

Are there any access hatches, say, to a loft? If so, note the size and ease of access. Is there a loft ladder, or room for one? Will you be able to get through the opening easily to store suitcases and unused furniture, and to get at the tanks?

Is the hatch cover hinged?

How is the opening trimmed? If there's a wooden surround it can look unsightly, but plaster that comes right up to the opening is easily damaged.

Floor

If there is a fitted carpet, you may have to take a lot on trust, but there is still a good deal that can be discovered.

Does it bounce or creak as you walk across it?

Is the floor level? Put a ball down and see if it runs.

What is it covered with? Floorboards are traditional, but may be uneven, and develop gaps. Check the direction in which they run, as a clue to which walls are structural. If parts have been lifted to get at the wiring, the panel should be fixed with screws; if you find this, take the opportunity of looking at the joists. If chipboard or plywood are installed instead of boards, you have a sound, even floor.

Are the floorboards sound and even? Look for soft and spongy wood, and for small round or oval holes that show a lighter colour inside, that might be a sign of live insect attack.

If it's a ground floor, is it solid (the finish laid on the site concrete), or suspended (constructed like an upper floor)? Recognise the latter by the presence of airbricks to ventilate
the space under the floor, which you will see outside the house.

If it *is* suspended, you should try hard to get a look under it. There is often an access panel made when heating was put in. Your torch and mirror will be useful. Don't be alarmed by signs of damp, so long as they're below the level of any timber.

Is there a clean concrete surface, with no litter on it, right across the ground? This is the oversite concrete.

Can you see daylight? You should be able to do so if the space is properly ventilated.

Is the timber sound? Look for holes on the underside, which show bright wood inside; for dust or pellets lying below timbers; for spongy wood; for wood which looks dry and seems broken into rectangular fragments; for what looks like masses of cottonwool; for fungi of any kind, especially red leathery areas with a creamy underlayer like sheepskin. If you see any of these, read Chapter 7, p. 144, carefully about what they may mean.

Note that timber which is stained green has probably been treated with preservative.

Floor covering

Examine the floor finish. Note carpet which will be left, ceramic or plastic tiles, or hardwood strip or block.

If there are fitted carpets, are there threshold strips to protect the edges at openings?

Are tiles firmly fixed down all over? Lifting tiles may indicate damp. Note the extent of the problem.

Are hardwood blocks lifting? If the floor seems hollow, this may be caused by them fitting too tightly, without the cork expansion strip that should run round the room. Look for this.

Is the surface of ceramic tiles worn? Quarry tiles, in particular, can be irrevocably damaged by injudicious cleaning.

Do you like the colour of the tiles? This is hard to change.

Space

The cost of replacing a piece of furniture with a less unwieldy one may be insignificant compared to the difference in price between two comparable cottages or flats. However, if it's a priceless antique or family heirloom you won't want to part with it, so you must check.

Thermal insulation

Be on the lookout for pointers to thermal insulation. Be especially vigilant:

- if wall surfaces feel cold indoors or warm (out of the sun) 113

outdoors when the heating system is running,
- if the snow on the roof melts before the neighbours',
- if the heating bills seem unreasonably high.

Also look for:

- at least 100 mm (4 in) of dry fill or quilt between joists in the roof space. If there is *none* a grant may be forthcoming to help provide some, but if there's any at all no help is obtainable. Many houses have about 50 mm (2 in).
- carpet underlays,
- paper stripping between gappy floorboards,
- draughtstripping to doors and windows,
- porches,
- double glazing (more effective than double windows).

Underlays and stripping are easy to add.

Sound insulation

If you suspect there might be a noise problem, look for:

- windows shut on a nice day (they may be shut against noise),
- nearby schools, motorways, railways, airports, factories,
- nearby places of entertainment.

If you see them, come back and listen at the time the problem is likely to be worst (even the end of licencing hours). Many people can get used to a rumble of traffic but will be wakened by a slamming car door late at night.

Double windows keep out noise better than double glazing.

If you think noise might be a problem between, say, flats, check the layout of the flats. You wouldn't want your bedroom next to, above, or below a living room. Terraced and semidetached houses are better if they're arranged with living rooms separated by halls, kitchens or garages.

Fittings

Good fittings often add a great deal to a house especially if they're contemporary with the building. Look out for: period fire surrounds; decorative plasterwork; stained and engraved glass, smoked glass, figured glass; staircases, balustrades, handrails, newel posts; conservatories and porches; sanitary fittings (if they're in good condition); kitchen fittings (if they're hygienic); panelled or veneered doors.

Features which add to convenience include: built-in cupboards (check for damp and rot), built-in wardrobes (especially if you have none), meter boxes with access from outside, remote control of main door in flats (with voice contact), delivery hatches allowing milk to be put into the house, coat cupboards in halls, dustbin stores, delft shelves, bookcases built into recesses; room dividers where two rooms can be used together.

Beware, however, of DIY 'improvements' which do little but demonstrate their perpetrators' ingenuity. Look carefully at standards of materials and workmanship. It's only an asset, too, if it's going to be useful to *you*.

Heating

Be sure that any system of central or other heating is convenient for *you*. In the case of flats, be sure you know whether heating is provided for the whole building or individual flats, and in the former case, how much control individual owners have over the level and expense. (See also p. 18.)

Find out what fuel is used, and what store there is if any, and what chores are involved.

Check the size of the store (it's cheaper to buy in bulk).

Ask to see last year's fuel bills.

Look for thermostatic and time controls on a central-heating system.

When was the system last serviced and the flue cleared?

Find the tanks, cylinder, boiler and check access to them.

Check the lagging of the cylinder.

Hot and cold water

Where is the boiler and how is it fired?

Are the pipes well lagged where no heat is wanted? Is the cylinder well lagged? Is there an immersion heater for summer use?

Is there plumbing for an automatic washing machine?

In addition to the above points, which you will have in mind throughout your tour, there are a few which apply to particular spaces.

Loft

The loft is simply roof space, generally used for storage, and usually contains important parts of the service installations. Careful study will give you important clues to the state of the roof. It is one of the most important parts of your investigation. Careful how you tread – if there are no floorboards there's nothing but plaster between the joists (apart from insulation) and you could easily put a foot through.

Look first at the underside of the roof slope. You may be able to see boarding (excellent!), the underside of the tiles, or felt. Don't be alarmed if felt sags – it has to, to let water blown under the slates or tiles run away to the gutter.

Check that air is circulating. If it isn't, the roof space will smell musty. Dry rot flourishes in musty conditions.

Look at the floor, if any. Are there even a few boards? They are very useful, not just for storage, but to avoid putting a foot through.

Look for dry fill or quilt insulation between the ceiling joists. Measure the depth (see p. 155).

Look with *great care* at the rafters and other timbers to make sure they are sound. Danger signs would include: sponginess of the wood (look for this especially near the eaves); small round or oval holes, especially if they show lighter inside; sawdust or pellets; any signs of fungus, especially reddish leathery masses with a creamy underside, cottonwool-like masses, wood which appears dry and broken into rectangular fragments. If you see any of these things, read Chapter 7, p. 144, at once to see what they may mean.

Wood which is stained green has probably been treated with preservative.

Check the size and shape of the loft to see whether it could at any time be converted into a habitable room: see Chapter 9, p. 166. Whether you want to do this or not, the presence of a convertible loft adds value to a property.

There will probably be a considerable amount of electric wiring visible. Examine this, to try to decide whether it is fairly recent. Modern wiring is usually plastic-sheathed, white, and fixed with clips. It is neat and smooth and easily distinguished from older, lead-sheathed cable. Where it passes through structures it should be protected by short lengths of pipe. Older, lead-sheathed wiring should be looked at by a qualified electrician to know whether replacement is necessary. Your notes on the wiring in the loft should be read along with those you make around the meter: see p. 120.

Look also at the water storage tank(s). There may be a cold water storage tank and additional headers for heating and hot water. Note the position and size of each (you won't be able to work out which is which until you have looked further at the whole system) and note the sizes and positions of pipes which are connected. Note specially the overflow pipes which protect the system and any pipes which discharge over the tanks. The ceiling insulation should be omitted under the tanks, and each tank should be lagged.

Look for any signs of damp from the tanks or at the eaves.

Attic

An attic is a roof space that provides living rooms. It should have plaster or some other lining to the roof slopes, a window and a proper staircase – a loft ladder won't do.

Check that the headroom is adequate (2·3 m/7 ft 8 in over half the floor space), that there is enough wall space to place furniture, and that the stair is safe, especially at the top. You should be able to stand upright at the top of the stair, and grasp the handrail before you start to go down.

If there are dormer windows, check that they are watertight.

Bedrooms

Check the sizes of recesses, especially the depth. A depth of half a metre (1 ft 8 in) is needed for a built-in wardrobe.

Does the bedroom door open so as to shield the view of the room? Is the door closer than 300 mm (12 in) to a corner? If so, it makes placing furniture harder.

Will the bed have to be placed along a wall? Is there room to pull it out to make it?

Is there a light switch that can be reached from the bed?

Landing

Is there at least 300 mm (12 in) between the nearest door and the head of the stair? Less is dangerous.

Is there manoeuvring space to get wardrobes into rooms?

Is there two-way switching for the stairs light? Especially important for the elderly, who need very well-lit stairs.

Bathroom

Are the fittings you want present? If not, is there room to put them in?

Is there room to bath a child or an invalid?

If you're elderly, are there handrails by the bath and WC?

Note the colour of fittings and tiles. Do you like them?

Is the floor finish watertight and washable?

Cylinder cupboard

Where is the cupboard? On the landing is better than in the bathroom.

How big is the cylinder? Look for a capacity of about 32 litres (7 gallons) per person.

Is the cylinder well lagged?

Note the positions and connections of all pipes. Feel them.

Is there an immersion heater for summer use?

How much room for linen is there?

Stairs

Are the stairs well lit by day and night? Important for everyone's safety, but especially the elderly.

Are there any winders or quarter landings? If there are, they're safer near the bottom of the flight. Single steps are considered dangerous: prefer a short flight of at least three.

Is there enough headroom so you don't feel the need to duck – and could move furniture easily?

Is the handrail firm?

Are there gaps anyone could fall through in the balustrade?

Hall

Is the front door glazed? If so, is there a horizontal rail? A large single pane is dangerous and if smashed might drop like a guillotine.

Is there a switch for the landing light?

Is there a front-door bell?

Is the letter box high enough to reach without stooping?

Is there room to move furniture?

Note the *size* especially. Excess space has to be heated and furnished, but too small a hall can spoil the appearance of a home.

Living rooms

Note especially the heating arrangements. Many families like a radiant heater as a focal point. Radiators thoughtlessly arranged can interfere badly with the layout of furniture.

Where would you expect to eat most of your meals? Are the arrangements convenient for this?

Are the spaces so arranged that more than one activity can go on at once?

Are you likely to disturb or be disturbed by the neighbours?

Kitchen

Is there an unbroken sequence of worktop/sink/worktop/hob/

worktop? This is a key point to the design of a kitchen, and very critical to its usefulness.

What is the height of the worktop? Is it convenient for *you*?

Can you reach the cupboards easily?

Make a particular note of the materials used on the floor, walls and worktops. Their durability, and the ease with which they can be cleaned, will be important to you.

Is there ample natural and artificial lighting, especially of worktops?

Is there any source of heat besides the cooker?

Can the windows be cleaned without reaching over appliances?

Give a black mark if the cooker is near the window. You can't have curtains or open the window while a hob is in use.

Is there ample storage, conveniently arranged?

Is there room for occasional meals?

Is there room for the appliances you will bring or buy?

Is there space for more than one person to work at once?

If you have children, is there somewhere, indoors and out, where they can play under your eye without being under your feet?

Conservatory/sunlounge

Does this provide usable space without detracting from other rooms?

Is there enough width to do more than use it as a store?

Does it have a glass roof, and if so is snow liable to fall on it from the roof of the house? Snow boards along the eaves would protect it.

Porch

Is the entrance with the porch, bell, light, letter box the one you would normally expect to use?

Is there room for a conversation under cover?

Garage

If it's built in, is the house/garage wall solid? Is the door heavy and strongly framed? Both are important for fireproofing.

Is it *really* a two-car garage?

Is there room for storage, work bench?

Cellar

If there's a cellar *always* inspect it. Be highly sceptical of any claim to have lost the key, and refuse to procede further until it has been found.

What is the headroom? Even if you'll only use the cellar for storage, you'd find it thoroughly inconvenient not to be able to stand upright.

Is it well ventilated? Chilliness doesn't matter: mustiness does. You should be able to see daylight from airbricks or iron grilles.

Is there any sign of damp? Especially crucial here.

Is there any sign of decayed wood? Look for dry, friable timber that seems broken into rectangular pieces; any sign of fungus or mould, especially reddish growths with a creamy underside, greyish masses like cottonwool; spongy wood; holes on the underside of timbers, especially if the wood inside the hole looks new and bright; dust and pellets lying below timbers, timber which sounds hollow when tapped, especially if dust falls out. If you see any of these signs, turn to Chapter 7, p. 135.

Meter stores

Is the electric wiring up to date? If new sockets have been put in without rewiring, this will be evident from the state of the wiring near the meter. Modern wiring is smooth, usually white. The fuses should be of the cartridge type, or there should be circuit breakers. You should be able to work out that the wiring runs to one or two ring mains rather than to each socket separately.

Can the meter be read without the reader having to disturb the household? This is especially useful if there will be no one in during the day.

For safety's sake, is the gas meter physically separated from the electric meter?

Shared areas, especially in flats

Is the standard of maintenance of the shared areas adequate? Find out the arrangements for maintenance, and the responsibilities of individual residents. It is also important to be certain that shared areas are kept in a condition with which you will be comfortable.

Look for any sign of vandalism.

Are there lifts? Are they working? Any block of three floors or more should have a lift and preferably more than one.

Do the stairs provide a proper escape route in case of fire? There ought to be an alternative escape route, and the two should be separated by doors that would stop smoke, and which are kept closed. If you are elderly or have small children, check that the alternative route is viable for *you*, and doesn't involve sliding down a chute, for example!

Are there fire hoses, or a dry riser, for fire fighting?

Is the entrance to the flat you're interested in overlooked? Some people would rather be able to talk to a visitor without being overheard, others would rather the entrance was supervised to some extent to deter burglars.

Is there access to private gardens, especially if you have children?

Is the main door locked at night?

Is there adequate parking space?

Does the postman visit each flat or only the main hall?

Exterior

Having completed your indoors inspection, turn your attention to the outside. This inspection, together with what you have observed in the interior, should give you the information you need to make a reasonable guess at the cause of any apparent defects.

Look at each face of the building in turn, starting from the top and working down. You may need to go across the road or to the end of the garden to get a good view of the roof.

If it's a block of flats, you ought to get a good idea of the general condition of the whole building – not only of the flat you're interested in.

Chimney

Is it vertical? Chimneys out of true are a hazard and can cause considerable damage if they collapse.

Is the pointing sound? See later, under walls p. 124, how to decide – but note that chimneys are specially vulnerable, and loose pointing here is a frequent cause of damp patches on · chimney breasts.

Is the 'flaunching' – the sand cement pointing round the pots – sound?

Is the lead flashing which protects the junction between the chimney and the roof in good repair and tucked in to a brick joint?

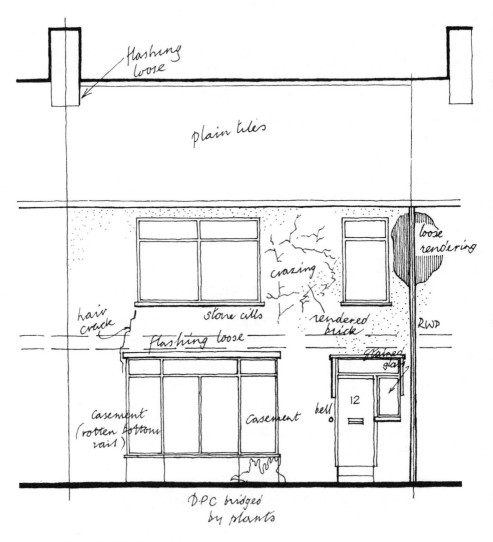

flashing loose

plain tiles

loose rendering

crazing

hair crack

stone cills

rendered brick

RWP

flashing loose

stained glass

12

Casement (rotten bottom rail)

Casement

bell

DPC bridged by plants

ROAD ELEVATION·

In need of decoration

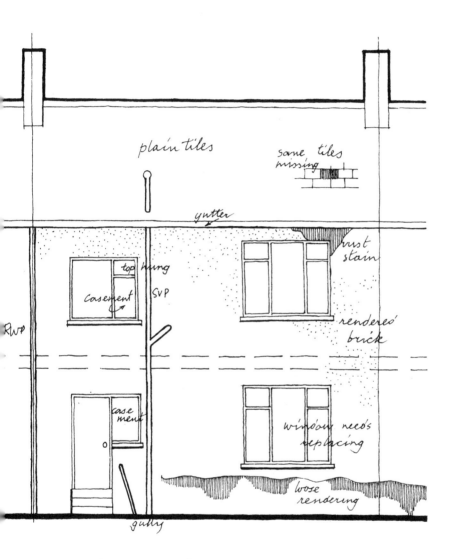

plain tiles

some tiles missing

gutter

rust stain

top hung

SVP

Casement

rendered brick

RWP

case ment

window needs replacing

loose rendering

gully

ARDEN ELEVATION

12 HAY LANE

Roof

For technical terms included below, see Glossary, p. 203.

If the roof is flat make sure you actually get up onto it. Check there are no puddles, that the rain water outlets are not blocked, and that there are no blisters in the covering. If there is a parapet, look to see that the flashings are sound (see above) and if there are eaves, check on the fascia boards – that they are sound, well painted, and firmly fixed.

If the roof is pitched, it is usually covered with tiles, slates or thatch, and the following questions apply.

Are there any slates or tiles missing or out of place, or bald patches? Water could get in, but repair isn't difficult.

Do you note any sagging, or are the courses and the ridge truly horizontal? Sagging might mean decayed or overloaded roof timbers.

Is the gutter in good condition, falling steadily towards a downpipe? If the fall has been lost, this might be due to mining subsidence or settlement for other reasons, so it could be an important clue if other defects are noted.

Are there any stains or rust marks where the gutter has overflowed?

Are the fascias and bargeboards sound and well painted? Try to see the underside as well as the top.

Are the soffitboards of overhanging eaves sound and well painted? If bits are missing, birds may nest in the roof – on the other hand, all ventilation to the roof shouldn't be cut off.

If the verges have no bargeboards, is the cement pointing sound? This is the only point at which cement/sand pointing should be seen on a roof: elsewhere this practice (it is known as 'torching') is to be deprecated.

If there are parapets or crowstepped gables, note any sign of cracking or damp stains.

Wall

What is the material?

Are there dressings of a different material?

Is the stonework clean? If it is badly discoloured, note also the appearance of any nearby buildings which have been cleaned, to help you decide whether this would be desirable.

Is the stone eroded? The surface of some stone wears away with the action of the weather, but this is rarely serious. The detail of carvings may be lost.

124

Is there any sign of white powder? This 'efflorescence' is unlikely to be important in itself, but may be part of a pattern of defects. Note how much there is.

Is the brickwork dirty or stained? It is rarely desirable to try to clean brickwork: you can cause worse trouble than you cure.

Has stone or brick been painted? This is highly undesirable, as salts may be trapped behind the paint, and damage result.

Is the pointing sound? If the mortar is powdery when you rub your finger along a joint, or if any part of the *top* surface of bricks is exposed, repointing may be necessary.

Are there any cracks? Note that these may be very fine, and as they usually follow the mortar joints they may be hard to trace. They often follow a diagonal stepped pattern: trace this carefully and record the line of the crack on your sketch. Include a note of the width, and especially of any difference in plane between the masonry on the two sides of the crack. Even small differences in width or plane can give important clues to the cause of a crack. You may find it helpful to draw small sketches of the whole building, with the cracks marked on in a very exaggerated form.

Where there is rendering or tile hanging, are the junctions with other finishes sound? Gaps in such positions are frequently the source of damp penetration.

Is there surface cracking or crazing, or is the rendering hollow?

Note lintols and arches over openings, and check that they are well supported.

Do cills shed water properly, or are there damp stains beneath? Look for the little grooves on the underside that should stop these.

Examine windows and doors for rot and the state of the decorations, as you did from inside.

Identify and trace the damp-proof course. In an older property this may take the form of two courses of blue bricks or slates, which would be clearly visible. Later property would have a thicker joint about two courses above the ground, where you could see the edge of the DPC. In modern work, the joint would be the normal size, but you should still be able to see the edge of the DPC. If you can't see it, there is a path for water to rise past it. Look also to see if the masonry is damper below than above this level. White or dark stains above DPC level may indicate the DPC is faulty.

Is the DPC 'bridged' by flowerbeds or rendering, which allow damp to reach the wall above it?

Are there airbricks below DPC level, and if so are they unobstructed? They ventilate the space below the suspended floor.

Are there any other air bricks? Older homes may have them either to provide ventilation to rooms or to supply a current of air to the void in cavity walls. Neither would be provided in modern building.

Try to identify any climbing plants or take a sample or make a sketch. Don't condemn all climbers, only ivies do real harm.

Identify any trees within 5 m (about 17 ft) of the building. They're probably doing no harm, but their presence *may* be relevant when you reach diagnosis stage.

Drains

You may shrink from the chore of examining the drains, but you can rest assured that this is most unlikely to be an unpleasant job. Begin by marking on your drawings the approximate position of all the fittings which have to discharge, as well as all the rainwater pipes. Find the ventilation pipe which rises above roof level and mark it, too.

Look for the iron or concrete access covers which show where the inspection chambers are. Lift these, taking care to put up barriers so that no one falls in. Get someone to pour soapy water down each outlet in turn, so that you can trace the drain connection, and make a plan. There should be no connections or changes in direction except at the chambers, so this shouldn't be difficult.

Does the water flow smoothly?

Do the open channels of the chambers look clean and sound?

You may find, in older property, that the last chamber before the sewer connection has an 'interceptor' in it, and a fresh-air inlet. These are now not used, as they proved to be a potent source of blockages.

Is there any sign of soggy ground near the drains?

If there is a septic tank, look especially for signs of leakage of raw sewage. It is expected that treated effluent will escape, but there should be nothing at all offensive.

External pavings

Look at the condition of all paths and drives.

What is the material? Is it sound?

Is it level or do puddles form?

126   Are the kerbs sound?

Boundaries

Your solicitor will let you know later which boundaries belong to and are the responsibility of the householder. You are interested, however, in the state of all the boundaries.

Are they pet-proof?

How high are they?

Do they provide privacy?

Are they in good condition?

Garden

Is it about the right size? If it's too big, you may be able to sell part to a neighbour; if too small, you may be able to buy more.

Are there retaining walls or ramps? These turn a sloping garden into a series of accessible terraces.

Can you see the garden from the living room, or even step out?

Can you see the garden from the kitchen?

Is there a pool? These are treacherous to toddlers and the elderly.

Are there perennial weeds?

Does the garden slope up from the house? You get a better view of the plot, but water drains towards the building.

Do you like the design?

Properties which have been altered

Many properties have already been altered when they are offered for sale. Check:

- that no overloads have been created, resulting in cracking,
- that no DPC has been bridged,
- that redecoration has been comprehensive rather than patchy,
- that matching materials and styles have been adopted,
- that the appearance hasn't been adversely affected,
- that all the necessary approvals have been obtained (you can ask to see the deposited plans at the town hall, building control department).

If the house you are looking at has been much altered, read Chapter 9 carefully.

Questions to ask

You are likely to have a chance to ask some informal questions of the vendor, so try to get all the information you can. The solicitor will ask any formal questions later. You might want to ask:

Why are you moving? (Perhaps they're getting away from the school next door!)

Which is the best school? Do the children from the road actually go there?

Is the public transport good? Maybe the frequent buses are full before they reach your stop.

Can we see the electric/heating/gas/rates bills?

Are you leaving the carpets, greenhouse, washing machine, etc.? Would you at a price?

Who made the alterations?

When was it last painted outside?

Have you tried for an improvement grant?

Don't expect them to tell you whether you'll like the district or get on with the neighbours. How could they tell?

Make a note of the questions you want to get the lawyer to ask, such as whether the road is going to be widened.

Surroundings

You will now find that you look at the surrounding buildings with new eyes. As you leave try to determine the general condition of them and see whether any defects you think you've found crop up elsewhere. This might aid a diagnosis. Notice signs of neglect or good upkeep.

All the information you now have needs to be mulled over. The next chapter will help you make sense of it.

Remember that you have not made a professional survey and will still need one.

Interpreting the results   7

You should now have amassed a large amount of information about the property you are considering. You have many clues to the age of the building, the way it is built and the convenience of the layout which you can best interpret for yourself in the light of the needs you have identified and the guidance of Chapter 2.

In addition, you have a good many notes and sketches of points which puzzle and perhaps worry you; things you suspect might point to serious defects though you can't be sure. You will need to weigh up carefully whether the house or flat is in so bad a condition that it isn't worth pursuing, or whether it is worthwhile getting a professional survey.

What I try to do in this chapter is to help you work out which of the clues might point to a fault serious enough to make you avoid the property altogether, which indicate the need for further enquiries and investigations, and which are less important but might lead you to seek a reduction in price to cover the cost of repairs.

Because diagnosing the cause of any fault usually involves putting together a whole series of clues, I cannot give you a simple list of causes and effects. What I do is list most of the things that might worry you, in an easily referred-to sequence, and discuss all the possible causes in each case. You will often find you are referred to another heading, but I have tried to keep that sort of cross-referring to a minimum.

The arrangement is as follows:

Cracks, bulges and leaning, p. 129
Holes, p. 134
Decayed and crumbling materials, p. 135
Stains, discoloration and bleaching, p. 139
Signs of damp, p. 140
Lichens, plants, fungi and moulds, p. 142
Smells, p. 146
Cold, heat and draughts, p. 146
Neglect, p. 147
Derelict property, p. 148
Property to avoid, p. 149

Cracks, bulges and leaning

You have careful notes of walls out of true, bulges and cracks. You now need to look, not only at these defects individually, but at the total pattern.

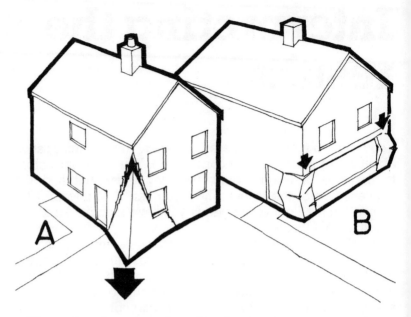

These drawings show how illuminating the exercise can be. In the case of house A, part of the foundation has given way. The exaggerated picture of all the cracks makes it quite clear that this must be so. On the other hand, house B has a pattern of cracks caused by overloading a wall when a new window was put in.

Looking at only one of the cracks, in either case, could have been misleading. Even an expert will be very cautious in stating what's causing such damage, and will usually want to observe changes over a period. The exception is that a surveyor practising in a particular district may know of faults which are particularly prevalent there, and be able to make a reasonable guess at the cause.

Long diagonal cracks

Long diagonal cracks, running from top to bottom of a wall, may be the most serious of all – and the most difficult to diagnose. It is essential to identify the cause and remove it *before* attempting a repair, as otherwise the crack will simply reappear. The commonest causes are those listed below: the symptoms are unfortunately often confusing.

Differential settlement

Investigation often shows that the ground under the building can, for one reason or another, no longer support the structure. This situation isn't uniform all around the building and so results in the building sinking unevenly. There will be cracking on more than one face. The drawing shows a possible pattern.

The cracks may apparently disappear at door and window openings, because they have taken the path of least resistance around the opening, reappearing above it. They rarely pass through arches or lintols. If an arch or lintol *is* cracked, it is because it is very firmly held in place by other structures. It will have to be replaced when repairs are done as it will no longer do its job of carrying the wall.

The causes of differential settlement include:

Loss of lateral support Building work on an adjacent site, even some time before, which excavated below foundation level may be the culprit. There is a common-law right to support from the site next door, so ask your solicitor to take it up.

Change in line of an underground watercourse could have washed away earth below foundations. Civil engineering work even some way away could cause this.

Mining subsidence In mining areas mining under property is a frequent cause of settlement. Mining first raises and then drops the land surface, causing great damage, but this happens once only and owners are entitled to compensation. Neighbouring buildings will most likely also be damaged.

Consolidation of the soil Houses are often built across old filled-in ditches. If this isn't done with sufficient care, the filling may settle after a time, leaving part of the foundations as an unsupported beam. It is very difficult to find evidence of this cause unless neighbouring property is also damaged, so that a pattern can be picked out across a whole estate. The fault appears within a few years of construction, and it may be possible to establish negligence by the builder.

Tree roots and shrinkable clay While recent research seems to show that tree roots do less damage than used to be thought, in 'shrinkable clays' which expand when wet tree roots can cause serious trouble. The cracks open and close with the weather. Note the presence of trees, or the stumps or roots of felled trees.

Frost The action of frost on soil extends to a considerable depth. In an exceptional winter the ground under foundations can be broken up, and its ability to carry loads reduced. This may show in cracking of the walls similar to that described above. Frost would be suspected where cracking first showed during the spring after a hard winter. Frost also causes the ground to heave, resulting in a pattern of cracking similar to that due to mining.

Investigation
Diagnosis in all the above cases would be aided by further 131

investigations. I suggest you cross check on the following points:

- can the crack be traced on both sides of the wall?
- is it clear from your sketches which part of the building is moving in relation to the rest? If so, where is the pressure being applied to cause this effect?
- is there any similar evidence on neighbouring property?
- is it a mining area? Ask the National Coal Board.
- what are the geological conditions? Ask at the town hall.
- has there been building work next door?
- has there been civil engineering work in the vicinity?
- are there any trees whose branches overhang the building?
- have any trees been felled?
- have there been any alterations to the building? If so, read 'overload' below.
- is there any sign of damp? If so, see damp, below.

Damage of the kinds described is always serious. You are unlikely to get a mortgage unless it's attended to, and it may take your surveyor up to a year to decide what needs to be done.

Besides removing the cause, expensive underpinning of the foundations will probably be necessary. See Chapter 8, p. 159.

Overload

Cracking which may be difficult to distinguish from that described above may be caused by additional loads which a structure wasn't designed to carry. There will generally be bulging or leaning as well as cracks – and in severe cases even collapse.

Two main mechanisms lead to overload.

Extension It's not uncommon for an extra floor to be added to a building. The foundations can generally cope, but the wall may not. It will probably buckle outwards.

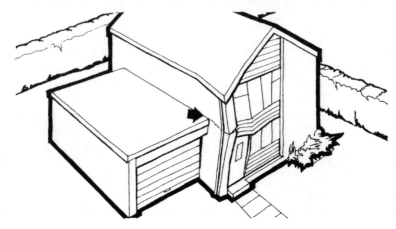

A single-storey extension may have half the roof load imposed assymetrically on an existing wall, causing failure.

Weakened wall If, say, a new window is made in a wall, this will weaken the structure, which may no longer cope with the loads put on it.

Investigation

If cracking is seen where there is evidence of alterations, suspect overload. Look for the point at which the excess load is applied, and try to see how else it could be carried. It will have to be supported before repairs can be done.

Work done in accordance with the building regulations shouldn't cause damage, so check at the building control department of the town hall that approval was in fact given. If not, there may be other dubious features.

Bulges

Any wall which bulges or leans is potentially dangerous. If it is more than one-third of its thickness out of true, collapse is regarded as imminent, so check this. Temporary shoring would be needed. Bulging is usually associated with cracking. As well as overload (see above, p. 132), it might be due to failure of cavity ties (perhaps due to corrosion); thermal or chemical expansion of something behind, pushing outward; failure of an intermediate support, such as decay of an upper floor.

Horizontal cracks, external

A crack which follows a brick course often results from different rates of thermal expansion in different materials. For example, a concrete roof may expand and push forward a brick parapet. A similar effect might occur along the line of the damp-proof course where the wall has a line of weakness. This is rarely sufficient to cause collapse. An external horizontal crack is difficult to correct because it's due to bad design, but it's generally not dangerous.

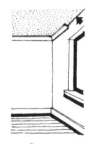

Horizontal cracks, internal

Horizontal cracks in plaster are often found near the tops of walls, especially in new buildings. They're not significant, and can be covered by a cornice.

Crazing

All-over crazing of plaster or rendering is usually caused by shrinkage during drying out, but might be due to chemical action between materials. It isn't usually important, though it's an expensive nuisance. Externally, the cracks will encourage damp.

Other Cracks

Minor cracking can also be caused by decaying timber, by rusting metal or by chemical reactions (see decayed and crumbling materials, p. 133). Vibration has also been blamed for generalised cracking in some cases.

Finally, cracks may be the result of poor construction, especially if they have appeared within a few years of building. Only assume this is the case if you have definitely eliminated every other possible cause.

Which cracks are important

Any crack which can be seen on both sides of a wall, which runs from ground to roof, which appears suddenly and any leaning or bulging ought to be treated as serious and investigated by a surveyor.

It is difficult to advise anyone to invest money in a property which has cracks of which the cause has not been definitely established. A proper investigation may take twelve months.

Claims for damages

In many cases, cracking is due to the actions of third parties, and it may be possible to make a successful claim for damages. However, it is always best for such action to be taken by the vendor, since he presumably held the property when the damage was done. If you buy a damaged property it could be persuasively argued that you had no case. If you want the house and can wait for it, get the vendor to claim and have the remedial work done to your satisfaction.

Remedial action for cracks is discussed in Chapter 8, p. 157.

The following conditions, which you might have expected to find under cracking, are dealt with under other headings:

lifting floor finish, p. 141.
peeling wall finish, falling wall tiles, p. 140.
dry, friable timber, p. 145.
crumbling masonry, p. 137.

Holes

Some gaps and holes are bound to arise between building materials, and some are deliberately introduced for ventilation or expansion. Holes you should worry about include the following.

Holes in roof Most of these are the result of dislodged tiles or slates and can easily be corrected. Try to determine how long water has been getting in, and be especially vigilant for signs of rot (see p. 116).

Holes in walls These may be the result of vandalism or accidental damage. If you think so, be wary of the district. If they result from erosion or defective materials the building is in serious disrepair (see p. 124).

Holes in ceilings Usually the ceiling has been brought down by water from a leak above (see p. 111).

Small round holes in timber These are important. They usually mean beetle attack – woodworm (see p. 135).

Decayed and crumbling materials See p. 135.

Mice Mice will colonise any cavity they can reach that's warm and dry. Eradicate the mice with bait: then fill their holes.

Decayed, crumbling and obsolete materials

Timber – see moulds and mildew, p. 145, and fungal growths, p. 144.

Beetle attack (woodworm)

Possibly one of the most important kinds of damage to timber is that caused by insect attack (woodworm).

Danger signs which should lead to suspicion of beetle infestation include:

- small round holes showing bright wood inside,
- a hollow ring to timber,
- 'frass' (the debris of chewed-up wood pellets and dust) lying beneath timbers.

Beetle attack is not confined to old buildings. It is very often brought into a property in second-hand furniture, or may be dormant in timber used in construction.

Furniture beetle (Anobium punctatum)

This insect attacks both softwoods and hardwoods, as well as wickerwork and plywood.

The adult beetle lays its eggs in surface cracks of timber. The grubs which hatch (understandably though wrongly known as 'woodworm') bore down into the wood, leaving behind pellets of chewed wood. Some of these may fall below the timber. The debris is known as 'frass' and is usually the first sign of an attack, though it may pass unnoticed. After anything up to three years, the grub becomes an adult beetle. It emerges, leaving behind the characteristic 'flight holes' which

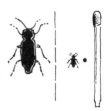

COMMON FURNITURE BEETLE
(Anobium punctatum)

135

most people recognise. These holes are round and small and if the attack is 'live' show clean wood inside. A great deal of damage, seriously weakening structural timbers, can be done before the attack is detected.

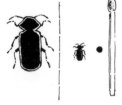

Death-watch beetle (Xestobium rufovillosum)

This beetle (not found in Scotland) has a life cycle which may be even longer than that of the furniture beetle. It is specially liable to attack old and decayed hardwood where there is poor ventilation. The flight holes are larger than those of the furniture beetle, and the frass contains bun-shaped pellets. A mating cry in the form of a gentle ticking may be heard.

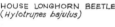
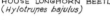

House longhorn beetle (Hylotrupes bajulus)

Although widespread on the continent, this pest is at present found only in a limited area of the south-west home counties, where its presence must be reported to the local authority and special precautions are in force. Attacks generally start in roof structures and work downwards, and the whole internal structure of timbers within a fragile shell may be destroyed. The beetle likes warmth, and may particularly be found near chimneys.

The flight holes are large and oval and the frass contains cylindrical particles.

Powder-post beetle (Lyctus brunneus)

This insect attacks open-textured, starchy hardwoods. The frass is a floury powder, and the flight holes are smaller than those of the furniture beetle.

Various other insects attack wood, but the damage they do is less serious as they die out of their own accord.

It may be possible to eradicate insect attack without replacing timbers, but this should not be relied on. You must obtain and follow the advice of a *reputable specialist.*

Do-it-yourself treatment is not advised.

It is reasonable to expect a vendor to put right damage of this kind or at least reduce the purchase price to pay for treatment. I would prefer the latter, as the purchaser has control of the work done.

If the vendor produces a guarantee as evidence that his property is clear of infestation, it is important to read this carefully and to understand exactly what it means. Usually such a document declares that, should an attack recur *in the timbers which have been treated* the firm will put matters right without charge. It may not cover a newly discovered attack elsewhere, it may specifically *exclude* visible woodwork, and it's only of value if the firm will remain in business throughout the period quoted, or has the backing of a trade association.

Check especially:

- the detailed specification, particularly the extent of the work,
- all exclusion clauses (these have been carefully drafted!),
- membership of trade associations.

A free survey for insect attack can be obtained from many specialist firms, and getting one is a sensible precaution in any house.

Rotten, spongy wood

See fungal attack, p. 144.

The structure of wood, particularly in unpainted windows, may break down completely, becoming blackened and soft. The condition may extend a long way down into the piece, which has to be replaced. Though this is occasionally called 'wet rot' it shouldn't be confused with fungal attack, and isn't infectious.

Warping

In well-seasoned timber the moisture content of the wood is equal to that of the building in which it is used, so that it won't warp. Warping may occur, however, if central heating is installed, or in wood very near to heaters. In most cases this is merely unsightly, though doors may have to be rehung.

Panelled doors which have been covered with plywood to make them flush may warp, because they can't 'breathe'. The best remedy is to remove the covering.

Stone

Erosion

Soft stones may show a worn surface caused by wind, rain and grit. This is rarely sufficiently serious to need attention and the use of paint or silicone surface treatments to limit further damage should be avoided. These only trap moisture and salts in the masonry, and may cause more serious damage.

Dirt

See staining, p. 139.

Brick

Erosion

The erosion of a brick surface can be more serious than similar damage to stonework, because many bricks have an applied face, which is removed leaving unsightly and hard to repair marks. Cutting out bricks and replacing them, even if a good match to the original bricks can be found, is laborious and often expensive.

137

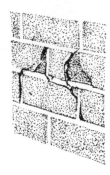

Surface spalling

Even more serious damage to bricks may result from the freezing of saturated brickwork. The expansion of freezing pushes the face off the brick, leaving a powdery surface. Again, impractical to repair and unsightly – but not harmful to the structure.

White powdery deposit ('efflorescence')

See p. 139.

Loose pointing

Where the mortar in joints is loose or powdery damp can get in, and the wall usually has to be totally repointed. This is a skilled and laborious job which shouldn't be postponed even though expensive.

Loose finishes (on tiles, wallpaper, rendering)

See p. 108.

Lead pipes

Lead water pipes should be replaced with copper (or plastic for cold water). The recovery value of the lead will go at least some way towards paying for the work. Lead cold-water pipes are dangerous because lead is a cumulative poison and slightly soluble in water.

Lead-covered electric wiring

This is a sign that the wiring is obsolescent. It should be checked by an electrician and may need to be replaced entirely for safety. All electric wiring over twenty-five years old should be checked every five years to establish that it's still safe.

Fabric-covered electric wiring

All fabric-covered wiring frays and becomes dangerous and should in almost all cases be replaced.

Plaster bubbling, powdery, loose from wall, etc.

The only remedy for defective plaster is to remove and replace it. It is usually necessary to decide what has caused the trouble (often damp, see p. 142) and remove it so that the problem won't recur.

Paint defects

See staining, p. 140.

Rust

Ferrous metals – on windows or pipes – which have rusted indicate the presence of damp (see p. 140) and also the breakdown of their protective covering. The damage may be so severe that the entire component has to be replaced.

Stains, discoloration and bleaching

Dirty stonework

In areas where there have been decades of atmospheric pollution, blackened stone is often cleaned to remove grime. As the deposits sometimes accelerate decay, this seems to make sense. Not everyone, though, agrees that a sparkling new surface is an improvement and cleaned stone darkens again fairly rapidly as the surface is slightly rough.

Various methods of cleaning are discussed in Chapter 8, p. 154.

Dirty brickwork

Brickwork should never be cleaned except for smoke marks caused by fire which can be gently removed with water.

Mortar stains on brickwork

It is very difficult to remove such stains without causing damage. DIY pointing may result in staining, making it a false economy.

Efflorescence

This white powdery deposit consists of salts which have been washed out of the brickwork by rain and have dried on the surface. In time, they will disappear, and they do no harm. Alternate hosing and brushing of the surface may speed their departure.

Dust and pellets

See beetle attack, p. 135.

Red spores

See fungal attack, p. 144.

Pattern staining

The pattern of ceiling joists is often plainly visible as light stripes across the plaster. This is due to the difference in temperature between joists and gaps, and may mean (if it's the top floor) that the roof insulation is inadequate.

Rust

See p. 138.

Bleeding through paint

Some resinous substances and bitumen tend to show through any paint covering unless a special primer is used. This looks bad, but isn't otherwise important. Strip down the paint, apply the appropriate primer, and redecorate.

Paint defects

Defective paintwork usually needs stripping off completely to eliminate the cause (often poor surface preparation).

Green stains

Structural timber stained green has been treated with preservative. Green stains on pavings, stonework and so on usually indicate moulds or lichen (see p. 142).

Damp stains

Determining the presence of damp is difficult, but establishing that a structure is dry is virtually impossible. While a reliable moisture meter will tell you what conditions are at the time it's used, if it's during a drought you have no evidence of what happens during torrential rain.

Signs of damp are usually unmistakable, and yet they may take many forms: dark irregular patches with lighter edges, light patches with darker edges or bleaching of wallpaper could all be the only evidence that the surface has been damp. Damp is almost always intermittent, and it's necessary to look for the damage it has done, since you can't guarantee to make your inspection on a wet day.

If you note staining of the kind described, especially if wallpaper or floor tiles are loose, or there are signs of rotting wood, it's essential to plot all the marks carefully so as to have the evidence on which you can make up your mind as to where the water is coming from.

If the building is new, remember that 'drying out' may take a year or more, and don't worry unduly if there is some evidence that this isn't yet complete.

Damp stains (as above) all round the building inside and out, at or just above ground level

This is reason to suspect the absence of a damp-proof course, or one that has been bridged by flowerbeds, rendering or pointing (in which case the remedy would be simple).

If there is no DPC – even in an older house on a well-drained site – it is very probable that no building society will advance money on it unless one is put in. There are various ways of doing this, see Chapter 8, p. 156.

Lifting ground-floor finish

This might indicate either that a floor finish which needs a damp-proof membrane has been put down without one, or that there is serious water pressure from below. In the former case you'd have to remove the finish and put down one better suited to the condition (e.g. ceramic tiles). In the latter case a damp-proof membrane, or even tanking, may be essential. See Chapter 8, p. 156.

Random damp patches on the inside of external walls

Rain water, as well as snow or fog, keeps up a persistent attack on the fabric of any building. It doesn't only fall – rain may be driven horizontally by the wind, and snow may drift. Few building materials are actually watertight; we rely on construction to stop water getting through them, and random patches of damp should be considered in relation to the construction used.

Cavity wall

Suspect that faulty craftsmanship has left deposits of mortar on the wall ties between the leaves, which are now providing a path for the water. The damp marks should appear within the period of the National Housebuilding Council guarantee, which should be invoked.

If the patches are near to door and window openings, suspect that the DPC at the closing of the cavity is missing or displaced. This is difficult to correct.

Solid unrendered wall

Check the wall thickness. If it is greater than 300 mm (1 ft) the damp may be due to loose pointing (see p. 125) or to a particularly heavy storm. Shrubs close to walls sometimes retard the drying out of walls, but climbing plants (except ivy) should not be sacrificed as they're unlikely to be the culprit. If the wall is thinner than 300 mm (1 ft) it may be essential to render it. Painted coatings on outside walls, either pigmented or transparent, may harm the structure by trapping salts and are best avoided.

Solid rendered wall

Rendering, such as roughcast, should be thoroughly inspected to ensure that it is adhering firmly (tap it to find a hollow sound) and not cracked or crazed. Faulty rendering attracts moisture by capillary action and then prevents drying out. Coarse renderings like roughcast are generally more effective than smooth ones like stucco.

Damp patches around windows

Windows are carefully designed, with small check grooves and projecting cills and drips, to stop water getting in. Sometimes paint builds up so that such devices cease to work as they should, and if water drips constantly on a wall surface it may eventually cause damp.

Water lying on the window board is more likely to be due to condensation.

Damp signs at roof level

If signs of damp are found at high level to upper-floor walls, it is likely that a blocked gutter or rain-water head is persistently overflowing, or that the water backs up above the level of the sarking and penetrates the roof space.

Stains above the level of lower roofs and bay windows

The flashings to lower roofs rise about 150 mm (6 in) above roof level, and are tucked into the masonry. If heavy snow builds up to a greater depth than this, and is melted by heat escaping from the building, it may penetrate the wall. Check, too, that the flashing hasn't come untucked, or been fractured.

Damp marks on chimneys

The flues of disused chimneys should be capped (leaving an opening for ventilation) to stop water building up inside. The pointing of chimneys is especially vulnerable.

Damp patches on ceilings

Although a stain may be due to a missing slate you should investigate the possibility of leaking service pipes or an overflowing storage tank. Damp may also come from condensation, especially in a kitchen or bathroom.

Damp patches on internal walls

These are almost invariably due to condensation. This can be definitely established by the use of a moisture meter, which can prove that only the surface is damp.

Blackened wood

See moulds, p. 137.

Lichens, plants, fungi and moulds

Lichen on roofs

Such growths in general do no damage, though they are a

symptom of age and their presence should lead one to examine the roof covering with special care.

Plant growths on outside ledges

These are usually rooted in deposits of dust and grit, but may damage masonry joints. Look for decay of the underlying structure.

Climbing plants

The majority of climbing plants enhance the appearance of a building without doing any damage at all, and it is a great pity that these are sometimes ripped off unnecessarily. Climbers fall into three groups:

- Plants which need the support of wires or trellis – make sure it's firmly fixed. Clematis is typical.
- Plants which cling by suction. These can be recognised by pulling a small tendril loose. They do no harm. Virginia creeper is one.
- Plants which climb by inserting their tendrils into the masonry. These *do* do damage, and should be removed. Ivy is the most serious.

CLEMATIS   VIRGINIA   IVY
                  CREEPER

Plants bridging the DPC

Plants close to a building may provide a path for water to a level above the DPC and so cause damp walls (see p. 125).   143

Adjacent trees

Few things make a nondescript house look better than a well-chosen tree, but the wrong trees in the wrong place can cause problems. Leaves block gutters, nothing will grow beneath the branches and roots may damage drains and foundations – see p. 126. It's a good rule of thumb that if a tree's branches can touch the roof, its roots can reach the foundations.

Fungus on external timber

This is unlikely to be actually dangerous unless there is already dry rot indoors, but it should be removed and the timber treated with a fungicide.

Fungus on internal timbers

Dry rot

The popular name 'dry rot' comes from the dry, brittle – and very weak – state in which the wood is left after an attack. It's possibly the term most feared by householders or prospective purchasers. However, if a thorough inspection is made by someone who knows what to look for, it is extremely unlikely that an established attack could pass undetected, and although treatment may be expensive and inconvenient, at least prompt action can eradicate it entirely.

Some people claim to be able to smell dry rot but it is more likely they recognise the characteristic smell of the fusty conditions which it relishes.

Danger signs include:

- red, leathery 'fruiting bodies' with an underside rather like cream sheepskin (or any other toadstool-like growth),
- any mass of cottony fibres,
- greyish strands or sheets across the surface of timber,
- dry, brittle wood which seems to be broken up into rectangular fragments.

Damp unventilated conditions are very conducive to rot. Examine any timber in such conditions with great suspicion.

Dry rot (*Serpula lachrymans*) feeds on unprotected timber. Red, dust-like spores drift or are carried into a building and if they settle on wood in damp, unventilated conditions, put out strands ('hyphae') which feed on the wood, weakening it. When the mass of cottonwool-like fibres is well established ('mycelium'), fruiting bodies ('sporophores') develop and further spores are released. The fruiting bodies look like big stalkless toadstools with dark, reddish tops. The fungus can put out thick strands to colonise fresh timber a metre or more away. The condition is virulent and exceedingly infectious.

Rapid treatment is essential. Insist on the vendor getting this done and passing you the guarantee. See remarks on guarantees on p. 154. Treatment is described in Chapter 8, p. 160, and is of course useless unless the source of damp is also dealt with, see p. 156.

Cellar fungus

Wood which has clearly been the subject of fungal attack, but which is in wet rather than damp conditions, may have 'wet rot' – cellar fungus (*Coniophora puteana*). This is less infectious than dry rot, but since it takes an experienced specialist to distinguish between the two, or to recognise other fungi which might attack, the procedure is the same.

In all cases you must have *specialist advice* on fungal attack, and follow it. *Do-it-yourself treatment is impossible.*

Moulds and mildews

Surface powderings or dark stains are often found, and if these are in a well-ventilated situation it is safe to assume that they are not virulent. They can generally be dealt with by swabbing with diluted household bleach, but as they are indicative of damp you should also seek out the cause and eradicate it.

Cottonwool-like growths and thick, grey strands

See fungus on internal timber, p. 144.

Cobwebs

See dirt, p. 147.

Smells

Drains, indoors

This is usually due to drawn or dried-out traps, especially in unoccupied property. Run water gently down the outlet, and the smell should disappear.

Drains, outdoors

The gully traps may have dried out, so try pouring water down. If the smell doesn't go, there may be a fractured drain, caused by traffic on an inadequate path or by tree roots. Local authorities will usually send someone to test drains, but if they have to be repaired it *must* be done by someone competent to the satisfaction of the local authority, and is expensive.

Gas

Always get the gas board if there's a smell of gas, and don't delay. It's dangerous to other people in the road as well as to the property in which it's found.

'Smell' of dry rot

This is mythical. See fungus on internal timbers, p. 144.

Cold, heat and draughts

Surfaces cold to the touch

A surface which is cold to the touch is liable to cause condensation and usually indicates lack of adequate thermal insulation. See Chapter 8, p. 155.

Surfaces hot (or warm) to the touch

This could be due to lack of lagging to pipes, overheated flue, *dangerous electric wiring*, solar gain.

To decide what's causing the warmth, consider the situation and extent of the area in relation to known flues, service runs and so on.

Draughts between floorboards

A great deal of heat can be lost through suspended ground floors. The gaps between floorboards should be filled, possibly with papier maché, though the circulation of air beneath the floor should *never* be cut off or a potential site for dry rot may be created.

Draughts in loft

It is far better to have a draughty loft than an unventilated one, providing there is good ceiling-level insulation and the tanks and pipes are well lagged against freezing.

Draughts in cellar

Encourage good ventilation in a cellar, but make sure that there are no gaps between the floorboards above.

Stuffiness

Adequate ventilation is essential, though actual draughts are undesirable. Air bricks and flues should not be blocked without allowance for some air flow, but it is no longer mandatory to have an air brick or flue in every room, so long as there are sufficient openable windows (an area equal to one-twentieth of the floor area of the room). Note, though, that if there are double windows and no flue the room may get stuffy. This is unlikely to be dangerous, because people would be uncomfortable enough to open a window before they were in danger of suffocation. Where there is a gas burning fire there *must* be a flue to remove unburnt gas.

Pay particular attention to the ventilation of rooms to be occupied by those who can't open windows (such as the infirm and children).

Neglect

Dirt

Dust and grit can be caused by broken-down surfaces; a build-up of food particles encourages bacteria; oil and grease can be dangerously slippery. Stains of any kind are unsightly.

Most dirt comes into buildings on feet, so lobbies with doormats at entrances are useful. It is also sensible if dirty areas like garages or kitchens are arranged to minimise the amount of dirt that spreads to the rest of the house, as well as being designed for easy cleaning.

Poor decorative repair

Paint on plaster is there purely for the sake of its appearance: paint on wood or metal is an essential protection. All wood that isn't painted should be varnished or polished, or impregnated with preservative. If no protective coating of this kind has been maintained it is important to assure oneself that the woodwork has not deteriorated beyond repair.

Look for a professional – or at least competent – standard of painting with even coats and neat edges ('cutting in'). Rough painting is liable to spoil subsequent work.

Fences

It is important that fences are properly kept up for security and privacy and to keep your own children and pets in and/or other people's out.

A fence usually belongs to the property on the side the posts are on, and there is an obligation on the owner or occupier to maintain it. Broken-down fences and gappy hedges can mean that the garden has become a haven for the urchins and dogs of the neighbourhood, who may be as hard to eradicate as any other pest.

Drives

A driveway should be strong enough to carry the weight of a car or van without damage to the drains which probably run beneath. If it is very uneven, these may be at risk. It should be reasonably free of weeds, but it is neither time-consuming nor expensive to get rid of these. (Children and dogs are best kept out of the way while it's done, as the chemicals are toxic.)

Paths should be even, and not so steeply sloped as to be dangerous when slippery. Steps should all be the same height, ideally in flights of at least three, and *must* have crisp edges.

Garden

It is unlikely you'd abandon an otherwise promising property because the garden was overgrown, but don't underestimate the difficulty of eradicating couch grass, dandelions or docks. See also p. 127.

Derelict property

If you are among the minority of househunters actively seeking a really run-down property that you can do up and sell at a profit, you need to examine potential buys with even greater than normal vigilance, though a recent report from the Building Research Establishment suggests that buying a really cheap property needing a lot of work actually makes good economic sense. A house with a problem is likely to sell at a greater discount on 'perfect' price than the cost of the repairs that are needed.

Also vet the neighbourhood thoroughly: you could lose money because the district was on the slide.

If a house is in a decent neighbourhood it should be worthwhile at least to investigate the cost of repairs (and the inconvenience and delay) before automatically writing off an otherwise attractive proposition. Ask yourself whether the work can be done before you move in (or whether you could put up with living on a virtual building site). Satisfy yourself that the refurbished building will, if not as good as new, be at least thoroughly liveable in when complete, and that its value will reflect what has been spent. See also Chapter 9.

Properties to avoid

I would suggest you avoid entirely any property where you would have to spend more than thirty per cent above the purchase price on repairs, unless its deliberately a rehabilitation project.

Also avoid:

- any property with structural cracks due to differential settlement or overloading, unless the vendor will pay for it to be put in order to your satisfaction,
- any place with signs of dry rot
- any place with active beetle attack

Be very sure you know what you are taking on in the case of property showing signs of any *two* of the following defects:

- no damp-proof course,
- one-brick external wall, unrendered,
- obsolete wiring,
- partial heating only,
- oil-fired heating,
- inadequate thermal insulation,
- damp due to bridged cavity.

Or any *three* of the following shortcomings:

- cracked sanitary fittings,
- defective plaster,
- dirt,
- overgrown garden,
- broken-down fences,
- shared areas poorly kept,
- potential noise nuisance due to poor planning.

You would naturally expect the price to be reduced for a building needing work. Beware, though, of the rock-bottom price: there may be another defect you've missed, or maybe no building society is willing to lend on the property.

8 Remedies to common problems

Even the worst problem is generally soluble, and even the most derelict property *can* be put in order – providing you can stand the cost and the upheaval. In this chapter I describe the remedial action that might be needed in various cases, help you to find out how much it will cost and discuss the help you might get from experts.

It is very likely that at some stage or another you will need expert help, but you may be bewildered by the wide variety of people to whom you could go. You may wonder, too, how seriously they would treat your problem – and how much their advice would cost.

If you need alteration work done you should consult a surveyor or architect if there is a problem to be solved. If the trouble and the appropriate remedy are clear cut, you might go to a builder, but remember that he is *not* trained to weigh up several possible answers to a problem and advise you on the best course to take. This distinction between 'professional' and 'commercial' advisers is one that it's best to be aware of: not because all professionals are disinterested and all business men are sharks – there are scoundrels in both camps as well as a majority of very responsible people – but because a man who is above all in business to make a profit for his shareholders is almost bound to advise you to follow a course *he* would find convenient to carry out for you, whereas a professional man is trained to survey the whole field of possibilities and recommend the one that would suit you best.

Builders are not necessarily any less talented, trained or experienced than their professional colleagues, but you don't have the protection of a 'code of conduct' which makes them answerable to a governing body of their peers, and you don't in the end save anything on fees because the price you are quoted naturally has to cover the time and trouble involved in advising you.

Professional advisers

The best way to find a reliable professional adviser is undoubtedly by personal recommendation. If this is not

150

available, seek the advice of the professional body concerned. (See Directory, p. 214, for list of names and addresses.) They will usually be happy to give you the names of two or three practitioners in your area who would be ready and able to undertake the work in question.

From the actual practices you should be able to obtain a firm idea of the fees you will incur and of how quickly they can do your work. If they are not able to give full attention to your problem at once, they will understand your need for speed and should be able to recommend a colleague.

If, after the initial discussion, you decide not to pursue the matter further you must expect nonetheless to pay a fee. A busy professional cannot give you his time for nothing, and he will probably charge you at a time rate for an initial discussion: £10–£20 an hour might be normal.

You will undoubtedly feel that there are some kinds of work that you could do yourself, thus saving what might otherwise be considerable expenditure on fees. I discuss this possibility, and give some guidelines, indicating especially the conditions in which you would really be out of your depth without specialist knowledge.

There are some general points worth bearing in mind.

An architect, surveyor or solicitor has the skill, experience and facilities that enable him to work very much faster than you would be able to do.

You will find many of these specialist tasks very time-consuming. If you put in the extra hours at your own job, might you in fact not earn more than the fees you are saving?

A professional has a duty to you as agent and can be held accountable if he fails to exercise a proper level of professional skill. If anything goes wrong this would be a valuable protection for you.

The professional institutions control and discipline their members, and ensure that only well-qualified people of probity belong. If you are dissatisfied you can protest to them.

On the whole, I believe that professionals give good value for money, though I do understand that if pounds are important this is one area where you may feel the necessary savings must be made.

Since you are charged according to the amount of time you spend with your adviser, you should prepare yourself thoroughly for the first and subsequent interviews. Arm yourself with all the information you will need, preferably set out neatly on a sheet of paper you can hand over. Your relationship with your adviser is a confidential one, so you need not fear giving away information.

Approach advisers confidently. After all, you are paying them. If you can't follow what you are told, say so and ask for an explanation. Make notes both in advance and during the 151 interview, and be prepared to confirm any important points in writing, keeping a copy of the letter.

These advisers are in law your 'special agents', which means that they have a duty to do a sound professional job and make your interests paramount for that particular commission. They are entitled to enter into agreements on your behalf, and you may wish to limit the area in which they can do so – especially financially – perhaps by defining the parameters in writing.

Architects

If you want to see the best way to improve or extend a house, or convert a property, consult an architect. He is trained to interpret your needs and solve problems for you, and he may be able to see possibilities you never dreamt of, so don't go along with full blown ideas of the alterations to be made.

Find him by personal recommendation or by asking the local branch of his professional organisation (the Royal Institute of British Architects) to give you a short list of firms who would tackle your job.

You pay according to a published list of fees, based on a percentage of the price of the builder's work, and you might find the fee came to 12% for alterations to a house. For this you would get full drawings, competitive prices from builders, and applications for council permissions, as well as supervision while the work was carried out to make sure it was all done in accordance with the standards agreed and priced for. If you just wanted to decide whether to go ahead with a purchase, so all you needed was to be sure that suitable alterations could be made (and how much they would cost) the architect would get out an outline scheme and give you a general idea of cost, and charge you according to the time he spent on the job.

The architect must by law have his name on the Register of Architects, and he is usually a member of the Royal Institute of British Architects, 66 Portland Place London W1N 4AD. Both the Registration Council and the RIBA discipline architects quite strictly. If you had any reason for complaint, you should

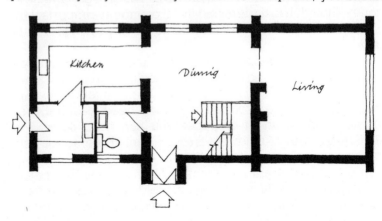

complain to them, and an architect who had behaved negligently might find his name removed from the register.

Surveyors

For advice on putting a property into good repair you could consult either an architect (see above) or a surveyor. See Chapter 6.

Legal matters

For legal advice and help over ownership matters or conveyancing, you are well advised to consult a solicitor, though (as described in Chapter 11) there are also specialised conveyancing firms, and of course generalised legal help can be obtained from the Citizens' Advice Bureau.

Financial advice

Your Bank Manager is generally the best person to turn to in the first instance for financial advice, since he knows most about your circumstances.

Commercial advisers

There is of course an enormous reservoir of expertise you can tap among people who offer their services on a commercial rather than on a professional basis. These include estate agents (see Chapters 4 and 10), specialised repair and improvement firms, and builders.

Builders

If you find you are going to need building work you may decide that this is straightforward enough for you to dispense with the services of an architect or surveyor, and decide to go direct to a builder.

It is usual, and sound practice to obtain competitive tenders for building work. Tenders differ from estimates in that they are actual offers to complete the work for a given sum, whereas an estimate may be more of a 'guestimate' of the amount the work might cost. In order that tenders should be genuinely competitive, it is essential that they should be based on exactly the same work, so a detailed drawing and description of the materials to be used and the conditions under which the work has to be done are needed. This is part of the service an architect would provide for you – and he would find the builders to tender. Don't expect a builder to find someone to make a drawing – he may be able to do so, but it would be a record and a drawing for getting approvals, not a basis for tenders.

153

It really isn't enough to walk round the site with each of the tenderers, talking vaguely about 'putting in a window' here or 'inserting a damp-proof course' there. These phrases could mean quite different things to different firms, and you would have no way of knowing what was included in any of the tenders when you got them.

Specialist firms

Many firms specialise in the provision of double glazing, the fitting out of kichens, the eradication of dry rot and so on. They generally have great accumulated experience of their chosen field, though they are happiest in fairly conventional circumstances. They may offer a 'design service', but you should note that this is more concerned with showing how their products would fit in to your home than with solving your particular problem.

In any of these areas there are enough rich pickings to attract cowboys, so great care is needed: the firms responsible for them can be difficult to identify. If there is a trade association, ask for their list of members, who they are likely to monitor. Ask, too, whether there is a scheme to indemnify the clients of firms who may go out of business or do shoddy work.

Guarantees

Guarantees that a problem won't recur, or promises to put right any further trouble need to be read with great care.

- They are valueless if the firm will have gone out of business before you want to invoke them.
- They may specifically exclude consequential damage, so that if, say, a faulty DPC is put right, you will still be left with damaged decorations to replace.
- It may be limited to that small part of the building which received attention, so that similar trouble occurring elsewhere is not covered.
- They may not be transferrable if the building changes hands.

Common problems

Cleaning stone

If you decide to clean blackened stone, choose the *gentlest method which will do an effective job*. All stone cleaning does at least some damage, and this should as far as possible be minimised.

The available methods, most of which have their own disadvantages, include water spray, steam, wet or dry grit blasting, and mechanical or chemical cleaning.

154

Don't just go straight to a stone cleaning firm – they might be specialists in a particular method of cleaning which is not actually the most appropriate in your case. Get advice from local experts – they will know not only the characteristics of the local stone but the nature and severity of local air pollution. The building control department at the town hall may be able to help.

Anyone considering cleaning a 'listed' building must consult the local planning authority and inform the Department of the Environment.

Cleaning brickwork

This should not be attempted excepting to remove smoke marks after a fire.

Improving thermal insulation

Methods of improving thermal insulation which are generally cost-effective include:

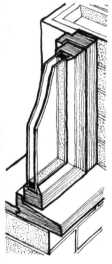

- Ensuring that there is at least 100 mm (4 in) fibreglass or other loft insulation. If there is none at all, a grant can be got to help pay for it, but this isn't available to improve the level. Many houses have around 50 mm (2 in).
- Carpet underlays.
- Milium curtain linings, which are nearly as effective as double glazing when the curtains are drawn, which is generally the case when it's coldest.
- Paper stripping (old newspaper will do) to the gaps in floorboards.
- Draught stripping to external doors and windows.
- A storm porch.

The claims of widely advertised and expensive methods, such as double glazing or cavity fill, need to be carefully evaluated for cost-effectiveness. Double glazing installed to keep heat in is most effective if it's true double glazing with sealed panes, not double windows.

Improving sound insulation

It is very difficult indeed to improve the sound insulation of a property, since this is really a characteristic of the way in which it was built in the first place. You have either to add a secondary structure (so that there is a whole double wall from foundations to roof, or a whole double floor) to prevent the transmission of sound through the structure; or to make the structure so heavy that it simply won't pick up the vibrations. The latter is generally pretty impracticable.

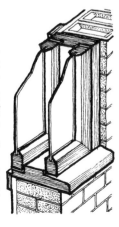

Double windows, with a gap of at least 100 mm (4 in) and sound-absorbant material in the reveal, are reasonably good at keeping out traffic noise.

Putting in a damp-proof course

If there's no DPC in a property the building society will almost certainly insist on one being put in before lending money. This can be done in various ways (by a builder or specialist; these aren't DIY projects).

Insertion

The masonry is cut out in short lengths to allow the insertion of short pieces of conventional damp-proofing material. This is slow and tends to be expensive, but is successful.

Injection

It is also possible to inject waterproofing compound into the wall. The disadvantage here is that as the fluid is virtually invisible it is impossible to tell how successfully the work has been done until it has been tested in practice, and it may be difficult to put a shoddy job right.

Electro-osmosis

By running an electric cable around the external walls an electric field is created which repels water. This is not connected to the mains or to a battery, but utilises the differences in electrical potential present in building materials and in the earth. This sounds like black magic but is said to work. It is quick to install and cheaper than the insertion of a conventional DPC, but the system has possibly been in use for too short a time for us to be certain that the effect lasts, and that the electrodes don't fail by corrosion.

Drainage tubes

The insertion of ceramic drainage tubes into the wall is generally considered less than satisfactory, though the technique may offer a useful second line of defence in combination with chemical injection.

Note that a particularly waterlogged site will be improved by putting in a system of land drainage to lead water away from the building. This isn't expensive, but needs to be done carefully to maintain a steady flow to the soakaway. You could do it yourself.

Tanking

Waterproofing accommodation which lies below the level of the ground involves installing 'tanking' very much like the waterproof lining of a swimming pool. A completely waterproof layer of material with careful jointing has to be put over the floor and the walls up to DPC level, and this then has to be protected from damage, and from being forced up by water pressure, by perhaps a half brick wall vertically and 75 mm (3 in) of fine concrete screed to the floor. I wouldn't try it yourself.

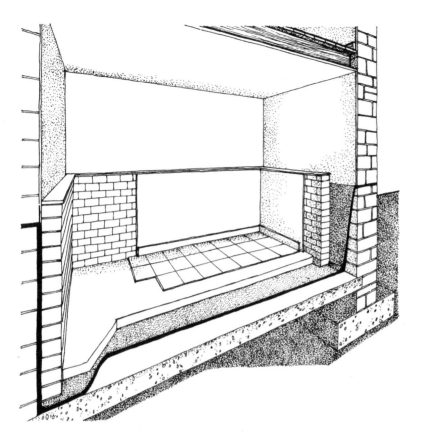

Tanking reduces the size of the accommodation, particularly headroom, and doors have to be altered and rehung. Care is needed with stairs, as the shallow step which will remain at the bottom of the flight could be considered dangerous.

Inserting a window

Very great care is needed to support the wall above a new opening during construction work, and I would suggest that skilled help is essential.

It is a simpler job if the wall is not load bearing (or carries only its own weight). You should be able to tell this from the direction of the floorboards and the construction of the roof. A lintol will, however, be required in both cases.

If the purpose of a new window is to improve daylighting levels it will usually be most effective if it is placed at a high level and at the opposite end of the room from the existing window. If it is intended to exploit a view, make sure that neither the cill nor any transoms will cut across eye level when occupants of the room are either standing or seated.

While a window may be a great improvement so far as the inside of the building is concerned, it can have a disastrous effect on the exterior. Make very careful sketches before going ahead to be certain that the effect is acceptable – the wrong 157

window, or a window in the wrong place is very hard to put right later.

It may be possible to get enough improvement in lighting without putting in a window by felling a tree and/or painting the walls of the room white.

Removing internal walls

Before attempting to open up the inside of a house by removing walls it is essential to know which of the walls are structural (i.e. carry the roof and floors above). Examination of the floorboards, which will run parallel to structural walls, should help you to tell. It is comparatively expensive to remove structural walls or parts of them, and temporary supports will be needed while the work is done. You will need experienced help. Non-structural partitions, on the other hand, can be removed in their entirety without difficulty. Services may need to be rerouted.

Adding heating

A building which cannot be efficiently heated throughout with a minimum of work is nowadays considered uneconomic: you would be buying accommodation you can't make full use of. You should, therefore, regard full heating as a necessary additional expense if you consider buying a property which hasn't got it already.

Get the advice of a heating engineer in professional practice: if you go to an installation firm you will probably find that they are agents for a particular manufacturer's boilers and so on, and they can't offer you all the options which are in fact available.

The decisions that have to be made will include one, choice of fuel: bear in mind storage requirements and the kind of flue required as well as cost. Two, whether to have circulated hot water, circulated warm air, or heated structures. The first of these means pipes and radiators where you may want to put furniture, but the components are nowadays small and unobtrusive. The second is usually difficult to put into an existing property as large ducts are needed. The third generally burns electricity (which might be enough to put you off the idea), and in the case of an existing building is generally a matter of putting in night storage heaters.

The commonest system is probably recirculated hot water, burning gas, of the kind described in Chapter 1, p. 19.

Electric rewiring

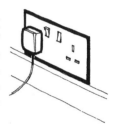

Electric rewiring *must* be carried out by a competent electrician. You should be prepared to pay for sheathing where wiring passes through structures and for ample thirteen-amp socket outlets, each switched. (It's little more expensive to put in double switched sockets than single unswitched ones, but this arrangement is much more convenient, and safer.)

Putting in a septic tank or cesspit

A septic tank will have to be constructed very carefully if it is to be acceptable to the local authority; a cesspit must be totally watertight. You are unlikely to get a choice: depending on the nature of the site, the authority will specify the type of installation you must have. For example, you wouldn't be allowed to put in a septic tank above a railway embankment.

This is a case for getting a competent local builder.

Repairs

Cracks

There are often two stages in the treatment of cracks:

1. During the observation period (which might be twelve months), temporary shoring will be needed to support the structure. The design of this shoring is technical and construction is specialised. *On no account* attempt the work yourself.

2. The cause must be removed and the damage made good. Many serious cracks are due to differential settlement, 159

necessitating underpinning of the foundations. This may be done by injecting grout below the existing foundations, by inserting a reinforced concrete beam, or by putting in short bored piles. The method chosen will depend on the nature of the ground – follow professional advice. The work is bound to be extensive and time-consuming.

Other remedial work for cracking may involve building buttresses or tying in a bulging wall to a floor structure with tie rods.

After whatever is necessary has been done, the crack itself can be pointed up, or, if this is considered unsightly, the wall may be wholly or partially rebuilt.

A purchaser finding serious cracking would be well advised to insist on the work being put right to his surveyor's satisfaction at the expense of the vendor. This gives a much better assurance that repairs are adequate than simply asking the vendor to carry out the work.

Fungus

If signs of fungus are found a specialist firm *must* be called in. They will do a full survey of the property, so far as it is accessible, make recommendations of work to be done and then guarantee that the trouble will not recur (see guarantees, p. 154).

The work they recommend will most probably involve removing and burning all the infected timber; sterilising by heat or fungicide all masonry in the vicinity; replacing all timbers removed by new members pressure-impregnated with fungicide.

Rapid treatment is essential.

Since dry rot or other fungal attack is a symptom of damp, the source of damp should also be traced and eliminated.

Moulds and mildews

These can usually be removed with diluted household bleach, but again the source of damp needs attention.

Insect attack

It may be possible to get rid of insects without replacing timbers, but do not assume this is so. The advice of a specialist firm is essential.

Masonry and timber will be sterilised with insecticide, and any new timber treated with preservative.

Improvement grants

You may be able to get financial help with some of the work discussed above. Improvement grants are described in Chapter 12, p. 195.

Alterations and Extensions

Very few of the properties that you view will turn out never to have been altered in any way. Most will seem capable of some improvement. Some, you will feel, are unsuitable as they stand but could be altered in one way or another to suit you.

Always proceed with caution before committing yourself to altering a house. Some properties are unconverted or unmodernised simply because it would be quite uneconomic or impractical.

However, it is worthwhile spending a little time and thought on examining what is possible: you may be able to buy and alter a property cheaply because you have seen possibilities to which the present owners and other buyers have been blind.

It is essential to begin on the precise lines set out in chapters 1 and 3. Your needs and the money available have not altered because you are considering a different way of fulfilling them. Measure the property as it stands against your needs, and its asking price against the money you have available, and you will be able to see what needs to be done and what you could afford to spend. Remember that an improvement grant may be available – one of your first moves should be to enquire about this at the town hall.

Also think carefully about how much of the work you wish and are able to do yourself. Read Chapter 8 on this point. Professional help to see the possibilities is probably worth the fees involved, and you may prefer to use skilled help with the actual work rather than do it all yourself. Work out how much you could earn at your own job in the time you would spend on the house – and how much longer it would take *you* to complete it than the experts.

Jobs you should not attempt alone without expert advice

Some jobs should *never* be attempted without expert help.

Never remove or put large holes in a structural wall. Work out which walls are structural by tracing the floor joists and rafters (floorboards run at right angles to joists). The walls which support the ends of these members are structural.

Never remove a corner of a building – always leave a short return wall.

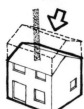

Never attempt to raise the roof.

Never attempt to lower the level of the lowest floor.

Never remove the lintol over a door or window opening, or the parts of the wall which support it.

Never excavate next to a building to lower than foundation level.

Most of these jobs are practicable so long as they are done by someone who not only has the proper know-how but also the right equipment, but they may be more expensive than you expect because of the temporary supports that are necessary.

Common types of alteration

The kinds of alteration that can be made to a house come under four headings: using a cellar, using a loft, making an extension, and total conversion of a non-residential property. The use which can be made of any of these altered buildings varies across the whole range of house functions, so if you want to add a bathroom, say, you will need to read the whole of the chapter in order to decide which is the most practical way, in your particular circumstances, for this to be done. You can also alter the uses of rooms without making alterations, or by removing walls.

It is of course not possible to give detailed guidance on designing or carrying out the work in the scope of one short chapter. All I attempt is to point out what the possibilities and limitations may be.

In addition to alterations which entail structural work, don't forget that changing the functions of rooms may make them more suitable for your needs. The possibilities here are virtually endless, but two possibilities are discussed: reversing the dining room and kitchen, and making a ground-floor bedroom and a first-floor sitting room.

Using a cellar

The basic difference between a cellar and a basement is that a cellar isn't regarded as habitable space: it may be damp, dark and ill-ventilated (though if it is it may constitute a hazard – see Chapter 7). If a space below the ground-floor level is to be used as living space, or even to store goods that might be at all vulnerable, it is essential to ensure that it either matches certain criteria or can be brought up to standard. As the space

is already enclosed, it might seem cheaper to do the necessary work to achieve this than to add an extension, but this is not necessarily the case.

You will need to consider the following points.

Is it dry?

One reason, before the days of damp-proof courses, for constructing buildings with cellars was to raise the main rooms above damp level. Basements are therefore often not used simply because they are damp. If you try to carpet or furnish a damp basement, the carpet will go mouldy underneath and your furniture will deteriorate, even if you are unaware of a sense of damp when you go in. You certainly will not get approval under the Building Regulations (see p. 174) to convert a cellar to living space unless you can show that it is dry.

A moisture meter is helpful to establish the presence of damp, but not infallible, because surfaces tend to be drier than the interior of structures. As discussed in Chapter 6, a moisture meter is invaluable in determining the extent of a damp patch, but unless readings are taken at intervals after torrential rain (up to many days, if the ground water level is significant) they are not alone sufficient to establish that a structure is dry.

You should assume, at least for the purposes of costing and comparison, that it will be necessary to put proper tanking into any cellar where this has not already been done, in order to make the space habitable. Chapter 8, p. 156, gives further information about this. Note in particular that both the headroom and the floor area will be reduced, the former probably by about 75 mm (3 in) and the latter perhaps by 150 mm (6 in) or more. Your DIY store should be able to quote typical costs per metre of the necessary materials.

If you have absolute evidence that the space is dry for all practical purposes – evidence that books stored there for several years have remained unharmed would be better proof than a few meter readings – you might be able to manage with no more than a sheet of heavy-duty polythene under the carpet and up the walls, which you could put in yourself, but personally I wouldn't risk any heirlooms down there, and the Building Inspector might be hard to convince.

Is the access adequate?

The existing access may either be a staircase, often of stone and very steep and dark, or through an external and rather constricted door or hatch. A converted basement is inconvenient to use unless there is reasonable access from inside the house, not only for people but also for the furniture which has to go down. Ideally the slope of the stair should be no steeper than 45 degrees, and the headroom measured at right angles to the slope at least 1·5 m (5 ft). If the present stair doesn't

measure up to these criteria, you may be prepared to put up with the inconvenience, or you may feel a new stair is necessary: is there room for one?

If the way in is at present through a door from the yard, or perhaps merely a hatchway, you may feel that this is unacceptable, and that a larger opening or a covered way is necessary. Either could be difficult and expensive to put in.

Lighting
The old criterion was that there must be a window in every habitable room equal in area to at least 10 per cent of the floor area. This no longer applies, but it gives a good rule-of-thumb guide to adequate daylighting.

If a new opening is necessary, it will involve a hole through a wall and a new lintol, as well as damp proofing round the opening. This may be a little cheaper and easier to do if the wall is non-structural, but at this level all the walks are carrying at least their own weight, so this is not terribly significant. A better situation would be an existing lintol over a coal hole or garden door, under which a window can be inserted. Expert advice is desirable, see Chapter 8.

Ventilation
It is essential to provide adequate natural ventilation in any 165

living space: an opening window of an area 5 per cent of the floor area would fulfill this requirement, or an unobstructed flue of equivalent size. Again, seek expert advice (see Chapter 8).

Drainage
It may be impossible to install in a cellar any appliances which need drains, unless the drains are even deeper than the cellar floor (check at the nearest inspection chamber). This frequently rules out using a cellar as a utility room, installing a second loo for use from the garden, or putting in a basin for a basement bedroom.

Hot and cold water and heating
Providing the capacity of the boiler is adequate (see Chapter 1) there should be no difficulty in extending water and heating services into a basement.

Electric
There is unlikely to be any problem in extending the electric circuits. If an additional fuse is needed for an additional ring main this will be easy to put in.

Thermal insulation
The heavy underlay under ground-floor carpets keeps the ground floor rooms warm, and the basement cool. Heat leaks rapidly from a basement into the surrounding ground, and you may need to provide a high level of additional insulation (see Chapter 8, p. 155). Your DIY shop should be able to tell you how much per sq m to allow for the materials.

Using a loft
A loft is the space surrounded by roof timbers above the highest inhabited floor of a building, and is generally used for storage and water-storage tanks. It is usually cold and draughty, reached only by a hatch and ladder, but dry. As it is enclosed space it may, like the cellar, invite conversion to living space: unfortunately this is often more complicated and expensive than anticipated. It is, however, a definite possibility, especially in town where ground space at street level is at a premium.

A number of factors need to be explored.

Is there sufficient space?
The Building Regulations, as well as your own convenience, demand that you should be able to stand up over a high proportion of the floor area of new rooms. The Regulations may require you to provide headroom of at least 2·3 m (7 ft 8 in) clear over 50 per cent of the floor area – and that is measured *after* any lining to the slopes of the roof and additional floor

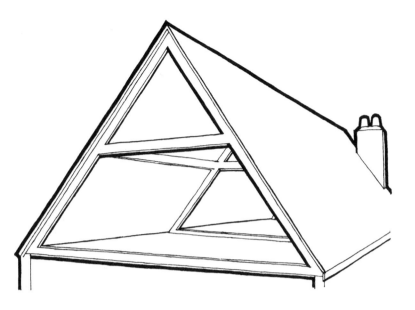

finish has gone in. You will also find that the roof structure constrains what can be done: there may be limited space between the trusses which effectively split the space up into separate areas, and you must not, of course, tamper with these. Modern roofs constructed with what are known as trussed rafters are virtually unconvertable for this reason, as well as having very limited headroom.

Access
The stairway to your new attic (and you are not likely to find a loft ladder is acceptable to the authorities) must be reasonably

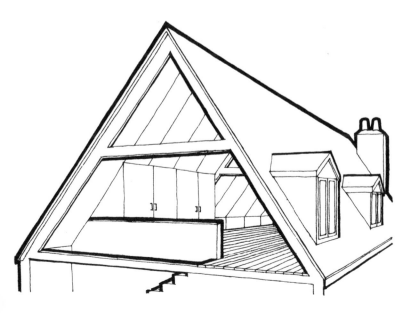

pitched (45 degrees); it must have headroom over it of at least 1·5 m (5 ft) measured at right angles to the slope, and enough headroom to stand up at the top (2 m/6 ft 8 in). The difficulty in accommodating this is likely to arise on the floor below the attic – some people find the only way to get good enough access to the loft is to sacrifice a room below. If there will be two rooms of a decent size in the attic this may be reasonable.

Natural lighting
You will need a reasonable level of natural lighting (10 per cent of floor area is a good rule of thumb, though no longer mandatory). This will involve either windows in gables (with lintols and weatherproofing) or dormer windows, which are rather specialised in construction. Dormers improve the headroom as well as admitting light. It is sometimes easier to get planning approval for dormers which overlook the back of a property rather than the street.

Ventilation
There should be no problem in providing good ventilation if parts of the windows are openable.

Electric
No problem is usually found in extending the electricity to the loft, even if an additional ring main is required (see Chapter 1).

Hot and cold water
It is often impossible to extend water services to an attic because of the limited head of the water due to the siting of the storage tanks. If the cold water is taken from the main, a cold tap may be possible, and if the storage tanks can be resited at the highest available point, hot water at fairly low pressure may be feasible. In any case, you will probably have to resite these tanks, since they will have been installed without regard to the use of the remaining space.

Thermal insulation
In most houses a most important part of thermal insulation is the quilt or fill which runs across the topmost ceiling, effectively minimising the rise of heat to the loft, which is therefore cold.

You will have to remove this and provide an equivalent layer of insulation to the roof slopes, where it is more difficult to fix and the range of materials available more limited. A material which is not vulnerable to damp must be chosen, and it must be fixed so that ventilation to the roof timbers is not impeded. Ask your DIY shop approximately how much per sq m this will cost.

Expert advice
168   There are firms who specialise in loft conversions and who

have, of course, a wealth of experience in these jobs. They have probably worked out efficient ways of working and may offer you little option as to the methods and materials they propose. If these suit what you need, well and good (but see Chapter 8, p. 154, before accepting a quotation). However, do not be browbeaten into accepting arrangements that are less than ideal because they suit the convenience of the contractor. If your needs are unconventional I would urge the desirability of consulting an architect (see Chapter 8, p. 152).

Extensions

Before deciding to extend a house it is wise to study estate agents' advertisements to ensure that you will get your money back when you sell. There is sometimes a ceiling on house prices in a particular locality which prevents this – people with more money to spend prefer a different locality or a larger original house. Try to find a property comparable to the one you have in mind which has already been extended, and compare the asking price with that of the house you are considering.(It would be worthwhile going to see this alternative property – it might avoid the need for inconvenient construction work.)

However, if you are considering an extension, it may be either because a house which really suits your needs simply doesn't exist, or because you hope to do the work at a later date when you expect it will be needed and expect, too, to be able to afford it. To make up your mind consider the following points.

Where can you extend?

The use to which you wish to put the extra space will have some influence on the position of the extension. Families often want to increase their total living space without necessarily adding to the number of rooms; they want one or more additional bedrooms; a larger kitchen or an extra utility room. There is no need to feel you must follow convention. Bedrooms can be on the ground floor, splendid sitting rooms can be made by throwing two bedrooms together, and kitchens don't need to be at the back of the house. However, convenience and the availability of services have to be taken into account, and it is common to add to living space by extending into the garden, to add to kitchen space by extending sideways, to add a bathroom by building out over a single-storey scullery, and to add a bedroom by building over a garage – to take a few typical examples.

Various factors will influence where you decide to extend. Consider the following points.

Building upwards

• It is essential to ensure that the existing structure is adequate 169

to support the additional loads. Expert advice is strongly recommended.

- The size and shape of the extension is limited by those of the supporting structure, which may be less than ideal. A single garage, for example, is often 2·5 m × 5 m (8 ft × 16 ft), which is an awkward shape to furnish as a bedroom.
- You must avoid obscuring important windows to the existing accommodation.
- Your neighbours' windows may have acquired a 'right of light' (see Chapter 11, p. 183) so that you must not obstruct them.

Building in front of the house

- There is probably a 'building line' set by the council, in front of which you are not allowed to extend.
- Planning approval is necessary in all cases, and you will have to convince the council of the attractive appearance of your proposals.
- It may be difficult to extend in this position without obscuring important windows.
- If the kitchen and bathroom are at the rear of the property, providing services for, say, a cloakroom may be tortuous.
- You must avoid allowing new foundations to bear upon the old ones.

Building sideways

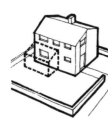

- The space may be limited, and foundations must be kept on your own property, so they will need in all probability to be asymmetrical.
- You will need to ensure that there is adequate access to the rear of the property for delivery of garden materials, window cleaners and so on.
- You will probably be building over drains, necessitating special precautions to relieve the load. If you build over an inspection chamber, you will either have to alter the drainage layout or provide a double sealed cover.

Building at the back

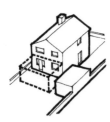

- There is a severe danger of obscuring important windows to kitchens and living room.
- Providing access to the extension may involve turning an existing room into little more than a passageway.

With any extension, it is vital to consider not only the extension, but also the effect it will have on the remainder of the building. In particular, make sure that the size of the extension is adequate, and that, unless it is intended as an additional area to an existing room, it has separate access and does not interfere with any other room, for example by obscuring a window. Careful drawings should be made, before you decide that any extension is viable. Follow the lines suggested in Chapter 5, p. 100, marking in the fittings and furniture you expect to use.

Conversions

If you are considering, as is increasingly popular, buying a non-residential building for conversion into a home, you will need to choose your property very carefully. Just because many rural railway stations and schools have been beautifully converted, this does not mean that every derelict property of that kind has the right potential. Indeed, if it hasn't already been snapped up you should ask yourself why that is the case.

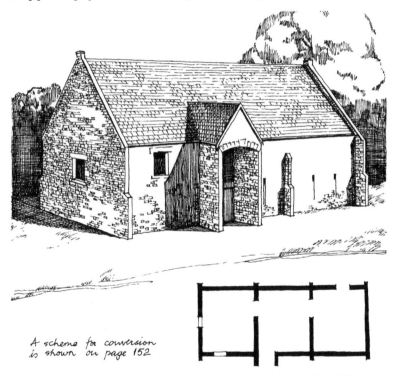

A scheme for conversion is shown on page 152

In choosing a place to convert, bear in mind the following points:

- Situation: if the building is inconveniently sited, it will never make a suitable home, no matter how delightful it may otherwise be.
- Total enclosed floor area and volume: however you intend to subdivide the space, you don't want either to be cramped or to end up with unusable space. Excessive headroom has to be either cut off by a well-insulated ceiling or heated.
- Availability of services. If there is no sewer, a septic tank is acceptable, if expensive. If there is no gas, other fuels can be 171

used. If electricity is unavailable, you may be able to generate your own. If there is no water you *must* ensure before committing yourself that a well can be sunk.

- Soundness of the structure. A proper and full professional structural survey is vital.

The charm of an old property can easily be destroyed by unsympathetic alterations. This is not to say that a pastiche on a historical style is necessary, but that the proportions and style of windows and doorways, the materials selected and decorative details should be carefully considered. You may feel that even your furnishings need to be adapted to the new situation.

Costs of building work

Read Chapter 8, p. 150, on the need for competitive tenders for building work: and Chapter 12, p. 203, on the possibility of obtaining an improvement grant.

It is very difficult to get any general guidance on the likely cost of alterations and conversion work. Someone in day-to-day contact with the construction industry may be able to hazard a reliable guess as to the cost of a new house – if size and construction are known – but you are unlikely to find anyone to do the same for alteration work. The only way to find out is to produce a detailed scheme and get in competitive tenders, making sure the contractors know they are in competition.

The reasons for the difficulty in estimating in advance include the following:

- Work undertaken to an existing building is much more difficult to organise and complete efficiently than work on a new building. This varies from property to property.
- If there are a number of small jobs to do in different parts of the building, this makes the builder's job harder.
- If the building is occupied while work is going on, the availability of constant cups of tea does not compensate for the difficulty of working around the family.
- Builders usually prefer to do larger jobs, all things being equal. Their eagerness to undertake your rather awkward work will, therefore, depend on the amount of work they have on at the time and expect to obtain. When there is little building work about, you may get a better price for alterations than when too much work is chasing too few reliable firms. In the latter situation you may have considerable difficulty in even finding a reputable firm to do the job. *Do not*, however, be tempted to get into the hands of cowboys. It would be better to see if you could build the job up to an attractive size, perhaps by cooperation with a neighbour?

- In trying to arrive at an estimate, bear in mind that actually getting the chaps and materials to the site and supervising them, costs virtually as much for a small job as for a larger one. Do not assume you are being held to ransom if the price you are quoted is far in excess of the total cost of materials and a reasonable hourly rate for labour. The builder has to maintain an office, clerical staff, telephones and transport, and pay insurances and holidays with pay, as well as borrowing capital – as you won't be paying till the work is done (see Chapter 12 p. 194). *Never* give the builder money in advance to buy materials – if he asks it means his credit isn't good.

Altering the use of rooms

It is often possible to make a house suit your needs better with only a minimum of building work. The example of a first-floor sitting room has been quoted (you may want to reduce cill heights to get a better view of the garden). The best way to think up ideas about this kind of alteration is to measure the property against your needs, trying to escape from convention into lateral thought paths. There are, however, two alterations which deserve special consideration here.

Kitchen/dining room swop

Changing habits have altered many people's expectations of their kitchen and dining room from those their grandparents cherished. We no longer attach so much importance to formal meals or imposing sideboards, we have many elaborate kitchen appliances which make demands on space, and these days we increasingly like to take informal family meals in the kitchen.

Many houses can be improved amazingly if the roles of kitchen and dining room are reversed. The new cosy dining space neatly accommodates the table and chairs, and the new roomy kitchen can be admirably laid out to suit our particular needs. So long as the house has a second door, there is no actual need for this to lead from the kitchen (indeed, it is far more difficult to lay out a kitchen well where this is the case). Although extended drains and rerouted services may be necessary, there is usually no need for structural work. And. there is no practical reason for the common practice of placing sinks under windows – this only makes such windows difficult to clean – so cill height need not be an inhibiting factor.

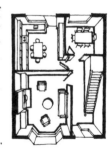

Ground-floor bedroom

Particularly for anyone disabled, a ground-floor bedroom is a decided advantage. It is only necessary to ensure that there is a downstairs toilet, and that a basin is installed (perhaps in a 173 cupboard, see Chapter 1, p. 10). If this can be done, a family with a disabled member need not be restricted to a single-storey house.

Planning permissions

Any alteration work whatsoever requires approval under the Building Regulations as well as town planning approval.

Building Regulations

The Building Regulations are an important protection from unsafe building for all of us, and even if applying and waiting for approval seems onerous, do not attempt to get round the rules.

Get the necessary forms from the building control section of the town hall. They will tell you how many copies of the form and of the drawings they need, what the fee will be and how long approval may take to come through – probably six weeks minimum, and don't start work earlier.

You can fill in the form and make the application yourself, though if you are employing an architect or surveyor he will do it for you. Unless you are a skilled draughtsman you probably won't be able to make drawings sufficiently detailed to satisfy the authority, and if calculations are needed of thermal insulation or the strength of lintols you may find you are out of your depth. I would suggest you consult an architect rather than go to one of the people who advertise 'plans drawn' under small ads in the local paper: the latter won't take any professional responsibilities or help you work out the best solution to your particular problem.

The actual work will be monitored by the local authority to make sure it's done in accordance with the approved plans and with any conditions that were set when approval was given.

Town planning approval

Quite separate approval is needed under the Town Planning Acts. The same department of the town hall will either be able to give you the forms or tell you where they can be obtained. Drawings showing the siting and appearance of the finished work will be needed, and there will be a further fee to pay.

Some categories of work are exempt, but procede on the assumption that approval is needed until told firmly that it is not.

Work which is exempt from planning control includes extensions at the back of property which do not exceed 70 cub m (50 in the case of terraced property). There are more detailed exemptions, about which you should enquire at the planning department.

In a 'conservation' area, or in the case of a 'listed' building, much more stringent rules may apply. Ask for details at the planning office of the town hall.

It is possible to seek 'outline' planning approval, to find out whether your proposals are likely to receive official blessing. This can be done quite simply even if you do not own the property. You then make a detailed application later, with full drawings, and wait for the approval to come before starting work.

London

In London, development is controlled by the London Building Acts rather than the Building Regulations. These cover the same general areas and are rather similar in their administration, but differ considerably in their detailed requirements.

Smoke Control

Under the Clean Air Acts, the government can make smoke control orders prohibiting the emission of black smoke and therefore, effectively, the burning of coal. Grants are available for the conversion of fireplaces.

10 **The decision to go ahead**

Settling on the kind of household you are, and the kind of home that would suit you can become an interesting game. Finding the property among those available in the right place and at the right price alternately fascinates and infuriates most people. The moment of truth when the far-reaching decision to buy and move must be taken may almost take them unawares.

It is imperative that you should avoid drifting into a purchase because you are weary of the search, because you feel you should snap up an unexpected bargain even without proper investigation, or because you've found a buyer for your present home and simply must have somewhere to go to. On the other hand, try not, if you have acted systematically, to have sudden qualms that you are in danger of making a mistake. At every stage you have acted thoughtfully, and you should not be tempted to question the basis of your early decisions at so late a stage.

The decision you are now making, however, is the most significant in the whole process. If you decide to go ahead and buy a particular, carefully chosen home, you at once commit yourself to considerable expenditure, it becomes important that you coordinate your actions with those of other people in the 'chain' of buyers and sellers, and you must either set aside considerable time for investigations and meticulous consideration of documents or else put yourself in the hands of a solicitor. You will also need to have various sums of money available at different stages.

For the purpose of this chapter, I shall assume that you intend to make use of all the expert assistance that is available.

Checking back

When you believe you have found the right property, you should, for the sake of your own peace of mind, take time to recall the stages of the whole househunting process, and measure your tentative choice against the criteria you established. This is necessary because it is virtually impossible that you will have found a home that matches your requirements perfectly from every point of view. You are bound to have to compromise somewhere, and you need to be certain that you are doing this in low-priority areas and not high-priority ones.

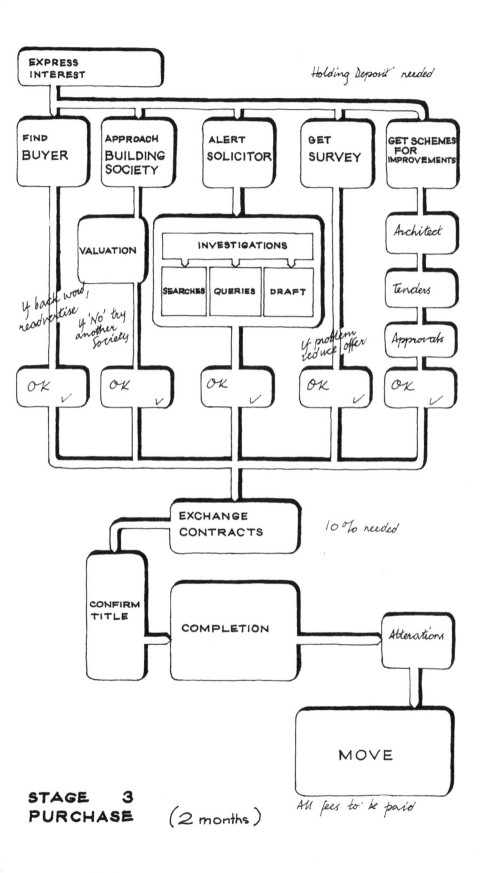

EXPRESS INTEREST

Holding Deposit needed

FIND BUYER

APPROACH BUILDING SOCIETY

ALERT SOLICITOR

GET SURVEY

GET SCHEMES FOR IMPROVEMENTS

VALUATION

INVESTIGATIONS

SEARCHES QUERIES DRAFT

Architect

Tenders

Approvals

If back word, readvertise

If 'No' try another Society

If problem reduce offer

OK ✓ OK ✓ OK ✓ OK ✓ OK ✓

EXCHANGE CONTRACTS

10% needed

CONFIRM TITLE

COMPLETION

Alterations

MOVE

STAGE 3 PURCHASE   (2 months)

All fees to be paid

Make a final check on the following points:

Is the accommodation broadly in accordance with the scale you decided on? Is the possibility of altering or extending available, if this is needed?

Is the accommodation arranged to suit your preferred life style?

Are the services you need installed?

Does the heating use the fuel your prefer?

Is the district right? Pay particular attention to this – it's the one feature of a home that's unalterable.

Is the building in sound structural condition? If not, can satisfactory arrangements be made for putting it in order?

Can you afford it? The price may include carpets and fittings which you have allowed for separately in your budget – or, perhaps, that you don't want but will have to buy. It's important to be sure you know exactly what is included. Ask about: carpets, curtain rails, light fittings, wardrobes, kitchen appliances, greenhouse.

Are you going to get vacant possession? You must be certain that teenagers and grannies have agreed to move out, and that there is no disgruntled spouse insisting on remaining during a matrimonial dispute.

Expression of interest

You would be well advised to avoid entering into any kind of verbal agreement with the vendor. You naturally hope that he will not find another buyer while you are formalising your offer, and it is reasonable to tell him that you are seriously interested and that your solicitor will be writing to him (or to his agent or solicitor). This makes it clear that you are a geniune buyer without any danger that a verbal contract on terms you did not intend could be held to exist.

If you intend to offer a price different from the asking price, you may wish to discuss this with the vendor, while he may prefer any haggling to be done by his agent. Make your offer in writing. It is absolutely essential to state that this offer is 'subject to contract' – so that if something untoward shows up in the survey the price can be amended, or if you have difficulty in getting a mortgage the offer can be withdrawn. Even if you are asked for and pay a holding deposit, there is no binding contract at this stage, and either party can renege. It is not unheard of for vendors to withdraw because they get a better

offer.

```
                                        5 High Street,
                                        Anytown,
                                        Loamshire.
                                        ──────────────────

                                        5th August 1983


    Dear Mr Nother,


    Thank you for showing us your house again this morning.  We
    find that it is very much what we are looking for, and we hope
    that we shall be able to buy it.

    I have been in touch with my Solicitor, Mr Smith of Smith, Grey
    and Partners, and he will be writing to you as well as arranging
    for the agreed holding deposit of £250 (which will, as we discussed,
    be returnable should the sale fall through for any reason) to be
    paid to your agent as 'stakeholder'.

    I have also asked Mr Jones ARICS of Jones-French, Surveyors, to
    carry out a structural survey on my behalf.  He will contact you
    to make a suitable appointment.

    I confirm that, subject to a satisfactory survey, and subject to
    contract, I am willing to offer you £33 500 for the property, to
    include fitted carpets and the curtains in the living room.


                                        Yours sincerely,


                                        John Bull.

    A Nother Esq.,
    2 Bluebell Lane,
    Newvillage,
    Loamshire.
```

Note that the holding deposit should *never* be paid to the
vendor, but to his agent or solicitor, who will place it in a special
account. You should make sure that it is held as 'stakeholder' for
the parties, and make it clear that it is to be returnable if your
purchase does not proceed *for any reason*.

Dispose of present home

If you have not already put your house or flat on the market, you
must do so without delay. Turn back to Chapter 4, p. 84. Your
newly acquired intimate knowledge of the market will make it
easier for you to set a price on your house.

Your aim must be to try to be ready to exchange contracts in
both transactions – selling and buying – on the same day (to
avoid having to have a bridging loan). You will probably find
that the people who are selling to you, and those to whom you
are selling, are in the same position.

179

If you are in rented accommodation, *on no account give notice* until contracts have been *exchanged*.

Apply for a mortgage

This is the stage at which you must follow up your informal enquiries about sources of finance (see Chapter 3) by making a formal application, in most cases to the building society with which you have savings on deposit, or the bank with which you have your account, and which your enquiries have shown you is most likely to offer terms which suit your circumstances.

If there is any difficulty, it shouldn't be impossible to discover whether the society or bank dislikes *you*, or dislikes the property, or simply hasn't money to offer at the time. Although they will have explained their lending policy to you earlier, and given you some idea of how it is likely to affect your case and the kind of home you have in mind, they will not begin their detailed investigations until you make a formal application for a loan to buy a particular property.

Since you will have enquired at more than one source, you should have a stand-by, so that you can approach another society if the first isn't forthcoming with an offer. The second will want to know whether you have applied anywhere else, and why you were turned down.

When shortage of funds at a building society means there is a waiting period, a different branch of the same society may be able to offer an earlier date.

Inform your solicitor

Exchange names and addresses of solicitors with the vendor, and let your solicitor have the name and address of the vendor's at once. Tell yours that you wish to make or have made an offer, and the amount, and he will put the purchase process in train.

He has very extensive searches, investigations and enquiries to make as well as the detailed fine tuning of the wording of the contract (see Chapter 11, p. 186).

Get a survey

You should now arrange to get a professional survey. Approach a surveyor practising in the area of the property: even if you have a cousin in the profession in the next county, the advantages of using a local man outweigh any saving you might get by going to a relative. You would also be embarrassed to claim negligence against a relation, so you might lose that important safeguard. See Chapter 6, p. 102.

Prepare schemes for improvements

If the suitability of the property depends on alterations or extensions being done before you move in, you will need to get in touch with an architect or builder straightaway. Designing the improvements can't be done overnight, and obtaining statutory approvals and competitive tenders takes several weeks. If work is to start directly completion is reached, preparations need to begin at once.

You are, of course, taking a slight risk that – should you withdraw your offer for some reason, or should the vendor go back on the deal – you might have to pay fees for abortive work. You will need to balance this against the importance of the work being done immediately.

Have money available

You may need to realise assets so that you have money available to:

- Pay the deposit (up to 10 per cent of the asking price).
- Pay for the valuation by the building society (on a sliding scale of up to £51 for a house costing £40,000, and by agreement for dearer houses).
- Your survey, based on the time taken (allow £150, and more if it's an older property).

These charges will have to be paid as they arise. There are of course other commitments you have now acquired, which will have to be met later. See Chapter 12, p. 192, for further details.

By taking the actions described you are initiating an intricate and lengthy process which is described in detail in the two chapters which follow.

At times you will almost despair because nothing seems to be happening. You no longer have the stimulous of the search, but have put your destiny into the hands of a great many other people – and you have to be patient. Because you know that deals *do* fall through, that snags in title *are* found, that vendors *do* withdraw, that your sale of your present home *could* break down, patience is very hard. You should realise, however, that the vast majority of sales are completed without difficulty, and that the delay is due to painstaking care being taken on your behalf.

11 The actual purchase

English law is constantly altering, as cases are decided and as new legislation is passed. No book can claim to be entirely up to the minute even on the day it is published, and one very good reason for using a solicitor is that his day-to-day work keeps him in touch with all the latest alterations. You will also recall that I made some comments on the advantages of consulting professional advisers in the course of Chapter 8, and these apply to legal matters as much as any others.

What I do in this chapter is, firstly, summarise some aspects of the law which are related to home ownership, secondly to describe the process of transferring ownership of a property from one person to another; and, thirdly, discuss the circumstances in which you might decide to undertake this work yourself, though I do not detail the stages and processes you would have to go through if you decided your case was sufficiently straightforward for you to do this. There are a number of books which describe this process in detail, and to which you could refer in these circumstances (see p. 189).

The home owner and the law

Ownership

Though a lawyer would insist that all land ultimately belongs to the Crown, for general purposes he would describe two 'estates' or types of ownership which, shorn of their legal jargon, are recognised as 'freehold' and 'leasehold'.

Freehold, for all practical purposes, describes land which can be willed or sold to others, and which is evidenced by title deeds which prove that there is no-one who can prove a better right to ownership.

Leasehold describes property in which similar rights have a time limit set on them. The period of ownership is usually paid for periodically in the form of rent. However, where leasehold property consists of a realisable asset, the payment usually consists largely of a capital sum called the 'premium', with the result that the rent is reduced to a low figure commonly referred to as 'ground rent'.

A piece of land, with a house on it, which is freehold, can still be subject to the rights of others. These are most likely to be covenants or easements.

Covenants

Covenants are conditions of use of land that are imposed by a vendor when he sells part only of his land. For example, where a house that is part of a new development is sold or where someone agrees to sell part of his garden. Common restrictions are that a single house is the most that is built on it, and that no business is carried out there. Such a condition would be binding upon any subsequent purchaser, but the right of a person to enforce covenants is often difficult to establish.

Other covenants could include an embargo on the hanging out of washing, a limit to the height of trees and fences, the duty to restrain pets – or indeed any other restrictive or positive rule the vendor liked to impose. (After all, if the purchaser didn't like it, he could look for land elsewhere!) If, however, you feel such a requirement is unenforceable or perhaps out of date, it is possible to apply to the courts for a declaration that it cannot be enforced, or to the Lands Tribunal to have it modified or discharged. A more practical solution may be to take out indemnity insurance which can be obtained upon payment of a once-for-all premium. If the risk of the covenant being enforced really *is* remote, the premium will be a fairly modest sum.

Not all covenants should be regarded as onerous. If a large area of land has been sold for houses, covenants may protect the rights of all the purchasers. You could be glad that your neighbour isn't allowed to run a business from his house.

The need to impose covenants has largely been superceded by town planning control.

Easements

Easements are rights which other parties have over your land (or vice versa), which may at one time have been granted or may simply have been acquired over the years. They include:

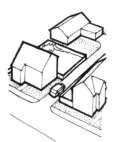

Right of way
The right of an adjacent owner to pass over the land may have been explicitly (or implicitly) granted when the land was sold, or it may have simply come into existence because the use of a covenient short cut wasn't challenged for many years.

Right of light (ancient lights)
This is the right a window can acquire for a reasonable amount of light to continue to fall upon it – not because the window is there, but because it has been unobstructed. A blank wall can't acquire a right of light, so you can't simply break a hole through one and then complain when a neighbour puts up an obstruction which blocks it.

There is no right to a view.

Right to support

A third common easement is the right to support from the property next door (not to be confused with the common-law right to support of foundations laterally from the land next door). This operates to make pulling down one house of a terrace impractical.

Easements which are not expressly created by deed usually only come into existence when the right has been enjoyed without interruption from 'time immemorial' (though in practice twenty years is often enough). They are *very* difficult to extinguish. Establishing their existence or otherwise is very complicated and supports endless litigation. This is not an area of the law into which the layman should stray unaided.

Restrictions of leasehold tenure

Covenants and easements can affect leasehold as well as freehold property, and in the former case there is the additional complication that, on the expiry of the lease, the land and any buildings on it will revert to the ownership of the ground landlord. The consequence of this is that leasehold property loses value rapidly towards the end of the lease, and it may therefore be difficult to get a mortgage for one.

There is a limited legal right for anyone who has owned the leasehold of a house (as opposed to a flat) for three years to buy the freehold. This means that if you bought the lease you would have to wait for that period before you could purchase the freehold: perhaps you could persuade the present leaseholder to buy, or the landlord may be willing to sell the freehold. There are conditions regarding the type of property, rateable value and the ground rent which have to be satisfied before the Act (the Leasehold Reform Act 1967) applies, but most leasehold houses held on a lease originally granted for a term of twenty-one years or more are encompassed by it. (For a full picture on this, consult your solicitor.)

In some parts of the country, mainly in the north of England, even some freehold property is liable to a rent charge or chief rent (which may often be bought out).

Registered and unregistered title

The title to land is proof that one person has a better right than anyone else to own it. Establishing that this is the case involves a study of the 'title deeds' which can be expensive and time-consuming, with the result that the system of registration of titles, whereby the state investigates and guarantees titles, has grown up.

The Land Registry keeps details of registered titles, though it won't allow these to be seen by all and sundry – you usually need to have entered into a contract to buy before the owner will permit inspection. In place of title deeds the owner of registered land receives a Land Certificate but, if it is mortgaged, a Charge Certificate will be issued to the building society or bank instead.

In many local authority areas registration is compulsory when land changes hands (the onus is on the purchaser).

The sale of registered land is normally cheaper and simpler than that of unregistered land.

Other responsibilities of house ownership

The owners of property have other responsibilities, including the following.

Party walls must be maintained, since the other owner may have a right to their support, and a right to enter and repair if you fail to do so. You must not allow loads from an extension to bear on the other owner's half. Certain statutory rules in London and Bristol are rather different from those elsewhere.

You must avoid causing a nuisance to neighbours. A nuisance is anything which interferes with his 'enjoyment' of his property.

You must not trespass on your neighbour's property. This includes letting branches from your trees overhang as well as letting your children scramble after errant balls. Your neighbour may lop off offending branches (providing he returns the timber and the fruit). Whether this applies to roots seems to be obscure.

You have a duty of care to visitors, including the postman and milkman (and even trespassing children, if you haven't taken adequate means to exclude them). If any of these are injured because your path is defective or slippery, they could sue you, alleging that you are in breach of the common law duty of care. Check your household insurance to see what cover you have against third party claims.

Boundaries

In the absence of other evidence, it is assumed that a boundary between properties runs on the *far* side of a ditch (beyond the hedge) or on the *face* of a fence (the posts being on the owner's land).

Control in the interest of the community

What you can do with your own property is also affected by Building Regulations, Town and Country Planning Acts and Smoke Control orders. These are described in Chapter 9.

The local authority

In many places in this book I refer to 'your local authority' or 'the town hall'. These terms vary in their meaning, depending on where you live. In general, if you are in any doubt as to which authority or which department wields the power on a particular 185

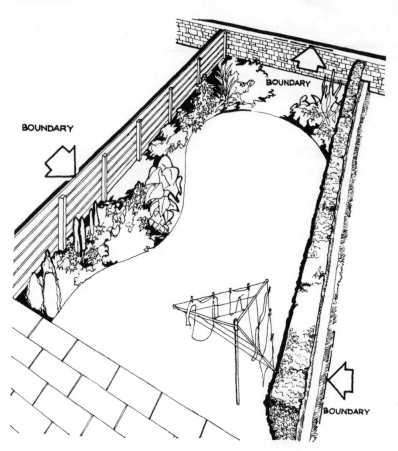

aspect of government, the simplest way to find out is at the local branch library.

Buying a property

The following section contains an outline of the steps your solicitor will take on your behalf in buying your house. He will consult you from time to time and the aim of this general guide is to help you understand what is happening at each stage.

Stage one: draft contract

The vendor's solicitor has the job of preparing the draft contract (he will usually use a standard printed form) which is sent to the purchaser's for scrutiny. If the vendor alerted the solicitor to the fact that he intended to sell when he made up his mind to do so, the firm may have started work on getting the title deeds from the building society, the bank, or wherever else they are kept, and the draft contract could be ready at once, but it usually takes a week or so at least for the draft to arrive.

The purchaser's solicitor examines this draft very carefully,
and will take the purchaser's instructions upon its terms,

perhaps sending a copy with notes on particular points he wants to draw attention to.

It is vital that the purchaser should read the draft carefully
Sign nothing at this stage
The draft will cover such points as:

- Names and addresses of the vendor and purchaser.
- Address of the property.
- A description of the property, defining the boundaries, mentioning any easements or covenants.
- A definition of what is included in the sale.
- The date of completion (this is normally left to be negotiated at the time of exchange).
- The price to be paid, and the deposit.
- The 'root' of title – a definition which proves ownership in the case of unregistered property.
- The capacity in which the vendor is selling.
- The rate of interest that will be due if payment is for any reason delayed (for example, if a selling 'chain' breaks down).
- In the case of registered property, the title number.

The draft contract might be accompanied by an 'abstract of title' in the case of an unregistered property and will be accompanied by a copy of the entries in the land register in the case of a registered property (all but the last sale price). In either case, this proves that the vendor really owns the place.

You are not strictly entitled to see the abstract until after the contracts have been exchanged, but you will be given details of everything (like an easement) that actually affects ownership.

The draft contract should refer to a plan attached to it, or to some document referred to in it, from which you should check the boundaries (and who owns them).

It's quite possible that you may disagree with some terms included in the draft contract, and feel they don't reflect what you agreed informally with the vendor. In this case, draw such points to your solicitor's attention, so that he can take them up with his opposite number. There may be quite a lot of minor alterations on both sides before the wording is finally agreed. Don't, therefore, feel that you *must* agree to anything you don't like – though you may have to compromise.

Pre-contract enquiries

At the same stage the purchaser's solicitor will make formal 'Enquiries before Contract', once more probably using a standard form, which includes many questions that may not be relevant to the particular case, but attempts to ensure that everything that matters has been asked. The vendor's solicitor is bound to reply honestly to all of these questions, as well as to 187 any special points that may be raised, provided they are matters of fact and not opinion.

Local authority search and enquiries
A search of the Local Land Charges Registers kept by the local authority is made prior to exchange of contracts (e.g. to check on smoke control, compulsory purchase orders). The result of the search should be carefully considered, but common entries such as smoke control orders are unlikely to influence your decision on whether or not to proceed.

At the same time, enquiries are made of the local authority to make sure that any road widening proposals, town planning restrictions and other intentions of the local authority which might affect the property are disclosed. The enquiries and search are made against the property itself and may not, as is commonly believed, provide any information about the immediate neighbourhood. Local knowledge and personal enquiries, discussed earlier (see Chapter 5) are therefore helpful.

Stage two: exchange of contracts
After the following conditions have been met, the contract may be concluded by the 'exchange of contracts'.

The source of money has been finalised.
The answers to all the enquiries and searches are satisfactory.
The surveyor's report has been accepted.
The draft contract has been agreed on both sides, including the completion date.

Once contracts have been 'exchanged' the parties are legally bound to go through with the sale, and there can be no further alteration of the conditions. Liability for insurance passes to the purchaser, but he doesn't yet get possession.

The purchaser also has to produce the agreed deposit (usually 10 per cent) which is paid to the vendor's solicitor, preferably to be held as 'stakeholder'.

Requisitions on title
It is possible for further questions to be asked at this stage, because it is only when contracts have been exchanged that you are legally entitled to see the deeds. The building society may wish to include questions in the requisitions.

Land registry search
If the property is registered, enquiries will be made by the purchaser's solicitor to assure himself that all remains as stated in the copy entry already supplied

Land charges register search

If the property is unregistered, the solicitor initiates a search of this register, to ensure, for example, that the vendor isn't bankrupt, that he hasn't previously agreed to sell the property elsewhere, or that he hasn't created a 'second charge'. A court order against him might show up here.

Final points

If there proves to be a legal snag to the sale at this point, the sale might still fall through, and you would be entitled to your deposit back, *if the fault is not on your side.*

One check at this point should finally establish that vacant possession is being given.

Stage three: conveyance and completion

The legal document which actually transfers ownership of the property from one person to another is not the contract but the conveyance; or, in the case of unregistered property, the transfer; and, in the case of leasehold property, the assignment.

This document is succinct, but sets out in legal terms the status of vendor and purchaser, the property to be transferred, the price to be paid and the date on which the transfer takes effect.

Receipt of the conveyance in exchange for the balance of the purchase price is what takes place at completion.

Doing your own legal work

There are two alternatives to employing a solicitor to draw up legal documents and watch over your interests generally during the purchase of a property.

One, you could go to one of the specialist conveyancing firms who offer a competitive service and with whom solicitors are nowadays prepared to work.

Two, you could do the work yourself, in which case you will need to devote very considerable time and concentration to the job, which is an intricate one.

There are a number of straightforward books you could refer to, if you are considering this last option, including:

Buckley, *Buying and Selling Your Home*, Owl Books.
Bradshaw's Guide to DIY House Buying, Selling and Conveyancing, Castle Books.
Giles, *Buying and Selling a House or Flat*, Pan.
Vickers, *Buying a House or Flat*, Penguin.
Which? Way to Buy, Sell and Move House, Consumers Association.

I would counsel you to think very carefully before denying yourself the benefits of professional advice and help. Certainly 189 it would be foolhardy to attempt a do-it-yourself operation unless:

- the property is a self-contained house,
- it is in England or Wales,
- the title is registered,
- it is wholly occupied by the vendor,
- it is freehold.

Scotland

The law in Scotland is very different from that in England and Wales, and you must not assume that the above applies there.

The financial   12
maze

In Chapter 3 I discussed the total financial commitment you make when you decide to buy a home, including running costs, to help you work out what purchase price you can afford. In this chapter I look at the payments you will have to make and when they will be due, so you can manage your cash flow as efficiently as possible. You need to keep considerable sums immediately accessible, you want to lose as little interest as possible on your deposits, and you want to minimise the amount you may have to borrow (particularly as a bridging loan) and the interest you have to pay on it. Check on the length of notice you have to give before drawing money out of your various accounts (the better the interest, the longer the period, often) and watch the stock market so as to be able to realise your investments (if you have them) at the most advantageous time.

Note that the same house costs widely different amounts in different parts of the country, so that what is actually an average price may seem ridiculously low to a Londoner and expensive to someone from the northeast. The building societies publish regular lists of the movement of property prices in various areas. These are helpful if you are moving from one part of the country to another.

The money you need will be required at four stages, now described.

1. Before you start house-hunting

Holding deposit

This deposit, paid to indicate your good faith at the outset, does not bind either the vendor or the purchaser, but it does give a sense of security because it indicates the seriousness of the parties. You ought not to go househunting unless you have some money for the purpose immediately available, because there is little point in it unless it is produced at once. You may be asked for something in the region of £250, but your offer is unlikely to be rejected if you offer less, unless there are a lot of potential buyers.

191

Valuation fee

Directly you ask a building society to consider lending money
on a particular property you will have to pay the fee for their
valuation. This might be £50 on a house valued at around
£35,000. Make sure you have it where you can get it at once.
Bear in mind that you may have to pay more than one valuation
fee if the first house doesn't satisfy the surveyor or the sale falls
through for some other reason.

Expenses of househunting

Unless you are moving within the same area, you will incur
considerable travelling and other expenses (see Chapter 3, p.
82). You will need ready cash to meet them. Allow for four or
more trips.

Selling

If you are selling a property at the same time, the advertising
charges may also have to be met at about this time.

2. At exchange of contracts

When contracts are exchanged, you should be prepared to
produce 10 per cent of the purchase price, even if you are
getting a 95 per cent or 100 per cent mortgage, although in such
circumstances a reduced deposit should be negotiated and is
frequently accepted. This should preferably be paid to a
stakeholder (see p. 188). The person buying your *present*
home is also likely to insist upon the deposit being held by a
stakeholder *so don't count on using the deposit put down on the
house you are selling towards the deposit on the house you are
buying.*

Estate agent's charges

The purchaser doesn't pay the estate agent, but if you are
trying to synchronise buying and selling, the bill from the agent
who sold your present home may arrive at about this time,
although agents don't normally look for payment until the sale is
completed: at least 1½ per cent of the house price.

Surveyor's fee

Expect the account from your own surveyor at this stage. As a
rule of thumb, allow £150.

3. At completion

Remainder of purchase price

On completion day, you will need your mortgage advance
cheque and any balance of the purchase price. Unless a chain

of sales can be very strictly synchronised, so that everyone in the chain hands over cheques or bankers' drafts on the same day, this may involve obtaining a bridging loan (see p. 195).

Stamp duty

Stamp duty at the current rate is payable by the purchaser within twenty-eight days of completion: roughly £350 on a £35,000 house.

Land Registry fees

Where the property is registered, or is to be registered, fees are payable to the Land Registry. These are due immediately after completion: roughly £88 on a £35,000 house.

Lender's legal charges

You will have to pay the building society solicitor at completion. Allow £122 for a £35,000 house if the society is using its own solicitor.

Removal charges

If, like most purchasers, you move on completion day, remember that you will have to pay the removal men in cash before they leave: for possible prices see Chapter 13. It is usual to tip them.

Incidental expenses

You will need cash in hand on the day you move for travelling, meals, and contingencies such as discovering that all the light bulbs have gone. If you are using a firm of removers, check that you will be insured against damage – but you will have to make arrangements at once to replace vital damaged goods, and wait to claim your money back later. Since you may be strangers in a new locality, you will need cash in hand to cope with emergencies.

The costs of a skip for the rubbish, of a plumber to disconnect/reconnect a washing machine and of putting a dog in kennels, for example, will have to be met on the spot. So will the fee for having mail redirected.

4. At completion or later

Professional fees

Solicitor

Your solicitor's account, which may include Land Registry fees and stamp duty, depending on his method of working, will arrive after a few weeks and ought to be paid without delay. Solicitors, unlike estate agents, do not operate according to a 193 scale of fees, but your solicitor should be able to give a reasonable estimate of his fees once he receives the draft contract and can see what is likely to be involved.

Architect

If you are having alterations made through an architect, his fees may become due in stages: when he has produced a scheme for you, when he has got in competitive tenders, and when the work is finished. The chances are, however, that he won't send an account for improvement and alteration work until the whole of the work is complete. It should be paid within the month. Allow 10 per cent of the cost of the building work.

Builder

It is usually to the client's advantage to agree to pay a builder in stages during his work. So, if you are having any building work done, you should be prepared to meet bills either whenever your surveyor or architect tells you that £x of work has been done or at, say, monthly intervals. Builders aren't in such cases paid for quite all of their work. About 10 per cent of the money is retained and not paid until absolutely everything has been completed to your architect's or your satisfaction (if you are handling the job yourself).

Since you won't normally get possession of the property until completion day, the builder can't start work, and therefore won't be in a position to be paid, until after that date.

Fees for statutory approvals will have to be paid earlier.

Services

You will get bills for gas, electricity, etc. in your old house, including disconnection charges, quite soon after the move.

The next bills for services at the new address will include reconnection charges. If you have not previously been a consumer of the service in question, the supply authority or the telephone authority will probably want a deposit from you.

Change of address

The printing and postage costs for informing your correspondents of your new address must be allowed for.

Money you may receive

Sale of present home

You may be relying on the money from sale of your present home to help towards the cost of the new one. But remember: *you will not be able to touch any of this money until completion day of that sale.*

Help from your employer

Employers who require their staff to move home usually help with the cost of the move. This may be limited to the removal firm's charge (and they may stipulate how many estimates you are to get and even from whom, so find out what the rules are at an early stage); or it may also include an allowance for disturbance. Where employees are required to move from the provinces to London, there may be an allowance to cover the difference in price of similar houses in the two locations.

Employers may provide bridging loans (see below).

See Chapter 3, p. 81, for mortgages provided by employers.

Bridging loan

Because of all the problems mentioned above, it is very common for families moving to find they need a short-term bridging loan. This is generally obtained from the bank at which they keep their account, and interest at rather more than the base rate, plus a fee for arranging the loan of around £20, has to be found. If at all possible, only get a bridging loan if you know for sure that it is for a limited period only.

Improvement grant

Improvement and 'intermediate' grants are given by local authorities to help owners bring property up to defined minimum standards. Money isn't paid over until the work is done, and no work must start until approval has been granted.

The authority may insist on more work being done than you actually contemplated, and as they will only pay a percentage of the cost (which varies from time to time and place to place) you could find it ends up being the opposite of a saving.

The local planning department or branch library should have leaflets giving details of the scale of grants available and the kinds of work for which they are given. For the purposes of the individual householder, they fall into three categories:

Intermediate grants, covering the installation of basic amenities like indoor sanitation in a house without it. The local authority is bound to give this, but can demand that you make a whole list of further improvements, so that the property measures up to their acceptable standard. The may also insist on repairs, and other conditions.

Improvement grants – these are discretionary, but can be given for a wide variety of work to properties below a specified rateable value.

Repairs grants – again discretionary, for repairs to houses and flats built before 1919.

If you are thinking of buying a flat or house which needs a great deal of building work, read Chapter 8, p. 150 on using professional advisers and getting a builder; and Chapter 9, p. 172 on estimating the cost, and p. 174 on planning approvals.

13 **Moving**

So you've exchanged contracts, the building society is happy, and the date for completion is set. Now you have to face organising the actual removal: an exercise in logistics to daunt even the most efficient.

The secret of an efficient operation, as with so many unaccustomed activities, is advance planning. If you think ahead, and start work early, there's no reason why you shouldn't find the challenge stimulating and the adventure enjoyable. Those families who collapse into their new homes determined never to fall victim to the temptation of uprooting themselves again are ones that never really thought out what was involved in the first place.

The operations breaks down into three stages:

1. Preparation

Arranging things in an orderly way so that they can be packed easily.
Disposing of things that won't be wanted at the new home.
Making arrangements for services to be cut off at one home and on at the other.

2. The move

Largely left to the removal firm, unless you are doing it yourself.

3. Settling in

Finding school, doctor, shops, etc.
Sending out change of address cards.
Arranging your belongings.
Finding the best routes, buses, train times.
Getting to know neighbours.

Throughout the process, you will find it's helpful to keep in touch with the people who are coming in as you go out, and the people who're going out as you go in. You will need to make arrangements about picking up keys; you may be able to avoid the electricity being cut off only to be turned on again; you can order milk for each other, and so on.

Preparation

Directly you know you are going

- Make a plan of what goes where in the new home.
  Decide what you're not taking and arrange to dispose of the
  rest. Sell what you can, through small ads, a garage sale, or

the local auctioneer. Take anything that has use left in it to the Oxfam shop or a jumble sale. Dispose of the rest to a tip or get a skip. Skips encourage you to clear out thoroughly. A miniskip (current price for a weekend, £12) may be adequate and do less damage if you have a drive. If a skip has to be left in the road it needs council permission and possibly lights, but the firm will arrange this.

Decide what you need to renew, and start shopping. Arrange delivery dates.

- Synchronise timings with the households coming in to your old home and out of your new one. If the place you are moving into is being left empty, you might be given access to decorate and so on. New carpets could be laid.
- Plan and get tenders for alterations and improvements (see Chapters 8 and 9).
- Run down oil or solid fuel and arrange to sell what's left to the new owner.
- Take cuttings from favourite plants (you're not allowed to uproot them).
- Find schools at the new address and take children to see them.
- Get bus and train timetables for the new district.

Removal firm

- Get tenders from at least three firms for the removal. Costs vary widely, and the degree of respect your possessions are accorded won't necessarily be proportionate to what you pay. The price will depend on the size of van, distance, and the number of men put on the job. Get tenders from firms in the new area as well as from some where you now live. They will need at least a week's notice of the removal date.
- Make sure you know exactly what is included in the tender:
  Will they insure even items they haven't packed themselves?
  Will they let you have packing cases for linen and books to stuff in advance – and how soon will they want them back?
  How will they arrange the timing (see below)?
  How much of the work will they want *you* to do (often strictly none)?
- Be certain that the people who come to look at your property before quoting for the move know all that has to be transported – the books in the loft, the plant pots in the greenhouse, as well as the furniture. If you're leaving the carpets, behind, for example, make that clear.
- Also make clear any peculiarities of your new home. If it's a third-floor flat with no lift, that will affect the price.

Do-it-yourself removals

The cost of a move is so high that doing it yourself is attractive.

You can hire a van (or better still, a van and driver) by the day and get friends and relatives at each end to help. Limit the amount of assistance you accept, otherwise you could spend more time telling people what to do than actually getting things done, and everyone will get in everyone else's way. You will need to provide fish and chips for all!

The disadvantages of the arrangement are that neither you nor your friends are skilled packers, so the job will take longer; you won't be indemnified against damage as you would by a firm; you (or a friend) might strain yourself lifting something heavy.

During the last two weeks

- Inform relations and friends, employer, old and new school, doctor, home helps, social services, National Health, National Insurance, income tax, bank, building society, hire purchase companies, professional bodies, trade unions of the date of your move and new address.
- Inform gas board, electricity board and Telecom of your move. Arrange for meters to be read at the old address and a service to be provided at the new address on the removal day. Try to cooperate with the other households involved over this, to simplify things.
- Arrange for cooker to be disconnected at old address and reconnected at new address on the very day of moving.
- Inform television rental firm, and ask whether you can take the set or whether they will install a similar one at the new address.

During the last week

- Get boxes from removers and pack books, linen, hobby gear, clothes, kitchen stores – in that order.
- Pack all drawers with knicknacks topped with linen to keep them firm.
- *Keep notes* of where you have put things.
- Finalise your what-goes-where plan. Give each room or space a number and code furniture and boxes accordingly.
- Return library books.
- Stop milk, newspapers.
- Make arrangements for granny, children and pets on removal day.
- Decide what you *must* take with you (as opposed to letting it go on the van) – e.g. the budgie, the silver, the monstera – and put it where it won't get put on the van by mistake.
- Put out a basic kit of kettle, tea, mugs, teatowel, toilet gear and first-aid kit where everyone can find it at all times.

Note that most removal firms refuse to take responsibility for china and glass unless they pack it themselves.

Removal day

You will have had to decide whether the whole move is to take place on one day, whether packing is to be on one day and unpacking on the next, or some other arrangement. You can often avoid having to stay overnight in a hotel or with friends by having all but the barest essentials put on the van one day, leaving little but beds to be picked up in the morning before an early start on the journey. What follows applies to the whole period of the move, whether it's all done on one day or not.

- Be ready early for the cooker to be disconnected.
- Expect meter readers early – and remember the services aren't supposed to be used once the meters are read.
- Keep children, old people and animals occupied and fed, or deliver them to friends, if this is what has been arranged.
- Put your basic kit (above) and the things you're taking yourself where they will neither get lost nor packed.
- Provide regular tea.
- *Don't get under the remover's feet.*
- Make arrangements to sweep out after the van has left. If the new people aren't coming in on the same day, you may be able to come back to do this, but it's often worthwhile to pay someone to come in to make sure you've left everything decent. Dispose of rubbish.
- Collect elderly, children and pets.
- Leave keys as arranged with neighbour, lawyer or agent.
- Get to new address ahead of van. You may find that you need to sweep out ready for your stuff to arrive.
- Put up plan of numbered rooms for easy placing of boxes and furniture.
- Provide tea
- Unpack boxes, though you usually needn't do them all. They will be left with you to unpack at leisure, and collected later by arrangement.
- Pay – usually in cash on the spot.
- Tip men – if you feel they've done a good job. 10 per cent of the cost of the move is normal.

Settling in

- Irrespective of the mess, get a good (takeaway?) meal directly the van has gone.
- Make up beds and put up bedroom curtains.
- Take time to unpack systematically. Start in the kitchen.
- Don't worry if you haven't got a presentable room. If neighbours drop in to welcome you they won't expect you to be tidy.
- Sign on with new doctor.
- Arrange for mail to be redirected. You have to pay £2 a

month. Hopefully the new occupants of your old home will do it free.

- Transfer your bank account.
- Get a new TV licence. These apply to premises, not people.
- Join clubs, library and so on, so as to get into the swing.
- Try out several new shops before deciding where to buy.

After a day or two you may feel a great sense of anticlimax. No longer keyed up with a deadline to work to, you have time to look around – and to notice in all clarity the disadvantages of the move. You miss the friendly neighbourhood newsagent who always had your paper ready for you, and you haven't had time to get to know the new one. You feel a stranger in the bus queue and the greengrocers. You recognise few faces and you're still finding your way about.

This feeling will pass, and with it the flood of nostalgia that accompanies it. You will begin to recognise the positive advantages of your new home, and enjoy the good points which made you choose it.

Because you took the time and trouble to identify just what would be, for you, a truly 'desirable residence', you can look forward with confidence to a long and comfortable occupation of the one you have chosen.

Good luck in it!

Glossary of the language used by Estate Agents

Estate agents are careful not to misrepresent the properties they offer for sale. They very naturally, however, present these properties in the best possible light, and they are skilled in the careful choice of words. The examples below are accompanied by the most unfavourable interpretations which may alert you to some of the devices employed. If a feature is ignored completely in a description, it's a fair bet that there was no possible way of presenting it as an asset.

Airy	Draughty
Bijou	Minute
Character	Usually means built prewar, but can imply eccentricity
Close to shops	Overlooking yard of butcher's shop/shoppers' car park/takeaway food shop
Compact	Shoebox
Conservatory	Draughty, leaking and probably rotting wooden porch
Convenient for schools	Next to playground
Convenient for transport	Bus stop outside/railway at bottom of garden
Cosy	Claustrophobic
Deceptively spacious	Looks even smaller than it is
Easily maintained	Modern capsule – you can dust the lot without moving
Easily run garden	Pocket-handkerchief plot
Elegant	Has all the fashionable features that will date
Enormous	Big
Exclusive district	The residents will only talk to you if you're the son of a duke/a scrap metal millionaire/a pop star
Extensive view	On top of a windy hill
Fully modernised	New sink/shelves put in by DIY enthusiast

Georgian style	Fancy dress attempt to make modern box look gracious. Doomed to failure
Good size	Just about bearable
Ideal for first-time buyer	No one who could afford better would look at it twice.
Individual	Full of the previous owner's odd ideas
In need of modernisation	Practically derelict
Lobby	1 m × 0·5 m (3 ft 4 in × 1 ft 8 in)
Modern	Built since 1935
Magnificent	Larger than average
Neat	Small
Offers scope for modernisation	Untouched
Offers scope for further modernisation	What little has been done hasn't been done very well
Older style	Built 1920–40
Park-like grounds	One acre of overgrown grass and shrubs
Popular area	Crowded district
Secluded	At the end of a narrow unpaved lane
Spacious	Bigger than average
Superior	Panelled doors and a coloured bathroom suite
Tastefully decorated	Yes – but whose taste?
Useful outhouse	Garden shed
Well appointed	Has the usual fittings

Glossary of Technical Terms

Air brick   A perforated terracotta block built into brickwork to allow air to circulate, say, below floorboards.

Ancient lights   An easement, right of light (q.v.).

Architrave   A timber trim which covers the joint between wood and plaster around a door frame.

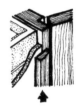

Area   A sunken space outside a building to allow light to reach basement windows.

Attic   Habitable rooms within the roof structure of a building.

Barge board   Timber trim to the verges of a roof at a gable.

Basement   Habitable rooms below ground-floor level.

Battens   Small timbers to which roof tiles, panelling and so on are fixed.

Bay window   A window which projects beyond a wall face, down to ground level but not usually up to roof level.

Beam   A horizontal member of, say, steel, which carries a load over a wide opening.

Boundary   The legal limits of a property.

203

Bow window — A window which curves outwards, generally set in a curving wall.

British Standard — A set of guidelines laid down, to which all well designed components should be expected to conform.

Building line — A line established by a local authority, in front of which no building work will be permitted.

Building Regulations — Rules to which all building work *must* conform, established nationally and administered locally

Casement — A side-hung opening light to a window.

Cavity fill — Thermal insulating material built or pumped into the cavities of external walls.

Cavity ties — Non-corroding twisted metal ties used to connect the two leaves of cavity walls.

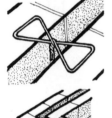

Cavity wall — An external wall made up of two independent leaves, usually one of brick and one of insulation blocks, with improved waterproofing and thermal insulating characteristics.

Cellar — Non-habitable accommodation below ground-floor level.

Central heating — Heating of a whole property from a single appliance.

Cesspit — A tank for the storage of drainage products, for removal by the local authority.

Chalet bungalow — A single-storey house with attic rooms.

Chimney — The structure which carries a flue above roof level.

Circuit breaker — A self-tripping switch incorporated into an electric circuit as a weak link, instead of a fuse.

204 **Clapboard** — American for weatherboarding (q.v.).

Cloakroom	A ground-floor toilet.
Combined system	A sewer and drainage system in which foul water and surface water wastes are carried by a single set of pipes.
Conduit	A round or oval tube arranged as a route for electric wiring.
Conservation area	A district designated by the local authority to have a special character or historical importance, and in which, therefore, special vigilance will be applied to planning applications.
Crow-stepped gables	Gables terminating in parapets with copings which do not run parallel to the roof slope and are often decoratively arranged.

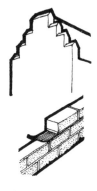

Damp-proof course (DPC)	A layer of water-resistant material nowadays built into all walls of every building to prevent the upward passage of water from the ground.
Damp-proof membrane (DPM)	A layer of water-resistant material placed across the floor area of a building to prevent the rise of ground water.
Development	Change of the use of land, which may or may not involve building work.
Double glazing	The fixing of two panes of glass, or a sealed unit with a cavity between the panes, into a single window frame.

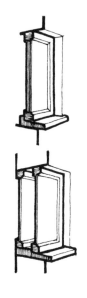

Double windows	The installation of independent secondary windows.
Earthing	Metal components and accessories of an electrical system must be connected to earth so that any excess flow is directed to the earth and does not cause electrocution.
Estate agent	A businessman who sells property on the vendor's behalf.

Facings		Bricks selected for their appearance, mostly used in external walls.
Fascia		A timber trim at the eaves of roofs, which often supports the gutter.

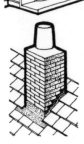

Fibrous plaster Preformed units, either in boards or in decorative features, made of plaster reinforced with textile, animal or glass fibres.

Fire surround A decorative feature built around a fireplace.

Flashing A piece of lead arranged so as to waterproof a joint between two structures, e.g. where a tiled roof meets a chimney.

Flue A carefully designed air passage which allows the creation of an upward draught either to aid combustion, or to remove the products of combustion or to improve ventilation.

Foundations The structures below ground which spread the loads imposed by a building to obtain adequate and even support.

Frass Dusty debris which may be an early symptom of attack on timber by insects.

Fuse A weak link, either of fine wire or as a cartridge, incorporated in an electrical circuit to detect and react to potentially dangerous overloading.

Gable The three-cornered end wall of a roof.

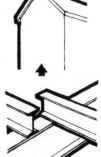

Girder A heavy beam which carries the ends of other beams.

Ground water
The water present below the surface of the ground.

Gully
A drainage appliance designed to receive wastes and convey them, through a water trap, to the drain.

Gutter
A preformed channel to direct a flow of water.

Header tank
A small storage tank needed on a hot water circulation to top up losses from expansion. Frequently combined with the overflow tank.

Hip
A sloping side roof used instead of a gable.

Hopper
A funnel at the head of a vertical rain water or other pipe, to collect wastes.

Immersion heater
A device to allow for the heating of water by the direct use of electricity.

Inspection chamber
A watertight chamber constructed in the run of a drain or sewer where there is a change of direction or a junction, to allow access.

Interception chamber
A chamber similar to an inspection chamber but provided at the boundary of a property to isolate the drains from the sewer, with an interceptor and sometimes a fresh air inlet. Found only in older property.

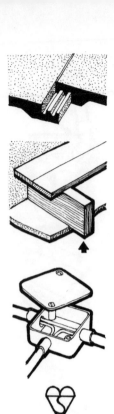

Interlocking tiles

Clay roof tiles which fit together along their long sides, eliminating the need for long laps.

Joist

A horizontal structural timber supporting a floor or ceiling.

Junction box

A box which connects electrical conduits, and through which access to the wiring can be obtained.

Kite mark

The mark indicating conformity to the relevant British Standard.

Lap

The overlap between one course and the next of roof tiling or slating.

Lathing

Metal mesh used as a basis for plastering.

Light

One panel of a window, which may be made up of several panes.

Lintol

A beam carrying a wall over a window or door opening.

Listed building

A building protected because it is considered to be of special architectural or historical importance.

Loft

A roof space used for storage but not providing habitable accommodation.

Mansard

A roof where the lower slopes are nearly vertical, making it easy to put in attic rooms.

Mildew	Powdery deposit of mould, symptomatic of damp.
Mould	Decay leaving a surface deposit on plaster or other organic materials.
Newel	The vertical post into which the strings of a stair are fixed.

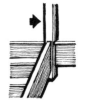

Overflow pipe	In a cold-water system, a pipe designed to cause a nuisance if the ballcock fails, to ensure that the fault is attended to.
Oversite concrete	A mandatory layer of concrete over the entire site within the external walls of a building.
Panelling	A wall finish of boards held clear of the surface by battens or framing and loose jointed.
Parapet	A wall which rises above roof level.

Party wall	A shared wall which separates adjacent properties.
Patio	External paving designed in close association with a house to provide outdoor living space.
Pitch	The slope of a roof.
Plain tiles	Nearly flat roof tiles of the traditional type.

Pointing	Careful filling of the edges of brickwork joints.

Preservation order	An order under town planning legislation to protect a tree or building.
Quilt	Usually refers to a layer of loft insulation laid across a ceiling.
Raft	A reinforced concrete foundation, used for light buildings on poor sites.

Rendering	A finish, mostly used externally, of cement and sand.
Retaining wall	A wall which supports higher ground on one side.

Reveal	The thickness of a wall 'revealed' at an opening.

Ridge	The top horizontal member of a roof structure.

Ridge tile	A specially made tile to cover the ridge of a roof.

Ring main	Modern electric wiring, with thirteen-amp plugs, to which as many sockets as desired may be added within a given floor area.
Riser	The vertical component of a stair step.

Rising main	The pipe between a water main and the storage tank.
Roughcast	A coarse-textured external rendering.
Sarking	A felt underlay to roof tiling.

Sash	A vertical sliding window light.	
Separate system	Drains and sewers in which rain water is carried separately from foul and water wastes.	
Septic tank	A small private sewage treatment plant requiring occasional emptying by the local authority.	
Settlement	The extent to which a building sinks into the ground: harmless so long as it's uniform.	
Shoring	Temporary supports.	
Site concrete	See oversite concrete.	
Skirting board	A timber trim to neaten the junction between wall plaster and floor finish.	
Small-bore heating	Heating pipes which are small in size and therefore unobtrusive, but whose use necessitates the pumping of the circulation.	
Soakaway	A specially provided area of underground rubble to which unwanted ground water or rain water can be channelled.	
Socket outlet	An electric power point, which should be switched and fused.	
Soffitboard	The boarding which lines the underside of eaves.	
Soil and vent pipe (SVP)	A vital pipe which accepts waste from a WC and is continued above roof level to allow sewer gas to escape from the system.	
Solid floor	A floor in which the oversite concrete (q.v.) directly supports the floor finish.	
Storage heaters	Heaters designed to provide a reservoir of heat obtained from off-peak electricity.	

211

Stucco	A very hard, fine rendering.
Switched socket outlet	See socket outlet.
Threshold	A raised timber to prevent the entry of water beneath a door.

Tie rods	Devices inserted into a building structure to improve stability after defects have arisen, (usually as cracking after differential settlement).
Tile hanging	Vertical external finish of plain tiles hung on battens.

Torching	Obsolescent and unrecommended pointing of roof tiles with cement and sand.

Transom	A horizontal member of a window frame, dividing lower from upper lights.

Trap	A pipe bent so as to retain water, preventing sewer gas from getting into buildings.

Tread	The horizontal component of a stair tread.

Trimmer	A structural timber which carries the ends of other timber shortened to create an opening (e.g. for a stair).
Truss	Structural timbers connected into a strong framework in triangular arrangements, usually to support a roof.

Trussed rafters	A modern roof structure, in which occasional trusses are replaced by rafters which are each connected into a triangular framework. This saves timber, but makes the loft space virtually unusable for storage.
U-value	A measure of the rate of heat loss through each square metre of a structure.
Underpinning	Permanent additional support for foundations.
Valley	A point on a roof where two slopes meet to create a gutter.

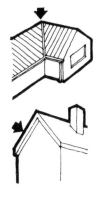

Verge	The edge of a roof at a gable.

Waste	(1) Discharge from a sanitary fitting. (2) The pipe which carries wastes from a sink, bath or lavatory basin to the drain.
Water table	The usual level of ground water below a particular site.
Weather- boarding	Horizontal timbers used as an external cladding. (Today the effect is often obtained by using plastic boards, which need no maintenance.)

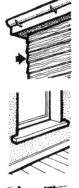

Window board	Internal trim to lower edge of window opening.

Window cill	External trim to lower edge of window opening, sloped to discharge water.

213

Names and addresses

For information, write to the following addresses:

Architects	Royal Institute of British Architects, 66 Portland Place, London W1N 4AD. 01 580 5533
	Architects' Registration Council, 73 Hallam Street, London W1N 1EE. 01 580 5861
Asbestos	Asbestos Information Centre, Sackville House, 40 Piccadilly, London W1XV 9PA. 01 439 9231
Boilers	Boiler and Radiator Manufacturers Association Ltd, Fleming House, Renfrew Street, Glasgow G3 6TG. 041 332 0826
Bricks	Brick Development Association (Advisory Centre), 26 Store Street, London WC1E 7EL. 01 637 0047
Builders	Chartered Institute of Building, Englemere, Kings Ride, Ascot, Berks. SL5 8BJ. 0990 23355
	Federation of Master Builders, 33 John Street, London WC1N 2BB. 01 242 7583
	National Register of Warranted Builders, 33 John Street, London WC1N 2BB. 01 242 7583
Building societies	Building Societies Association, 34 Park Street, London W1Y 3PF. 01 629 0515
Cavity fill	National Cavity Insulation Association, P.O. Box 12, Haslemere, Surrey GU27 3AN. 0428 54011
Concrete	Cement and Concrete Association, Wexham Springs, Slough SL3 6PL. 028 16 2727
Damp-proof courses	British Chemical Damp-Course Association, 51 High Street, Broom, Bidford on Avon, Warcs. B50 4HL
Decorators	British Decorators Association, 6 Haywra Street, Harrogate, Yorks. HG1 5BL. 0423 67292
	Interior Decorators and Designers Association, 45 Sheen Lane, London SW14 8AB. 01 876 4415

Electrical	National Inspection Council for Electrical Installation Contracting, 237 Kennington Lane, London SE11 5QJ. 01 735 1322
Estate agents	National Association of Estate Agents, 21 Jury Street, Warwick CV34 4EH. 0926 496800
	Incorporated Society of Valuers and Auctioneers, 3 Cadogan Gate, London SW1 0AS. 01 235 2282
	Royal Institute of Chartered Surveyors, 20 Lincolns Inn Fields, London WC2A 3DG. 01 242 0403
Fire	Fire Protection Association, Aldermary House, Queen Street, London EC4N 1TU. 01 248 4477
Glass	Glass and Glazing Federation, 6 Mount Row, London W1Y 6DY. 01 629 8334
	Safer Glazing Information Service, 44–50 Osnaburgh Street, London NW1 3DN (ex-directory)
Insulation	Structural Insulation Association, 45 Sheen Lane, London SW14 8AB. 01 876 4415
	EPS Association, P.O. Box 103, Haywards Heath, Sussex RH16 2JZ. 0449 57871
	See also Cavity fill, above.
Insurance	British Insurance Association, Aldermary House, Queen Street, London EC4N 1TU. 01 248 4477
Law	The Law Society, 113 Chancery Lane, London WC2. 01 242 1222
	HM Land Registry, Lincolns Inn Fields, London WC2A 3PH. 01 405 3488
	Oyez Publishing, Oyez House, 237 Long Lane, London SE1 4PU. 01 407 8055
	Stamps Office, Room 239, Bush House South West Wing, The Strand, London WC2B 4QN. 01 438 7039
Loft conversion	Loft Conversion Advisory Bureau, 594 Kingston Road, London, SW20. 01 542 9095
Mortgage brokers	Corporation of Mortgage Brokers, 24 Broad Street, Wokingham, Berks. RG11 1AB. 0734 785672
Paint	Paint Research Association, 8 Waldegrave Road, Teddington, Middlesex TW11 8LD. 01 977 4427
Plumbing	Council of British Ceramic Sanitaryware Manufacturers, Federation House, Station Road, Stoke-on-Trent ST4 2RT. 0782 48675
	Institute of Plumbing, Scottish Mutual

215

	House, North Street, Hornchurch, Essex RM11 1RU. 04024 51236
Removers	British Association of Removers, 279 Grays Inn Road, London WC1X 8SY. 01 837 3088
Roof coverings	Association of British Roofing Felt Manufacturers, 69 Cannon Street, London EC4N 54B. 01 248 4444
	British Ceramic Tile Council, Federation House, Station Road, Stoke-on-Trent, ST4 4RU. 0782 45147
Surveyors	Incorporated Association of Architects and Surveyors, Jubilee House, Billing Brook Road, Weston Favell, Northampton NN3 4NW. 0604 404121
	Incorporated Society of Valuers and Auctioneers, 3 Cadogan Street, London SW1X 0AS. 01 235 2282
	Royal Institution of Chartered Surveyors, 29 Lincolns Inn Fields, London WC2A 3DG. 01 242 0403
Tiles (floor)	British Ceramic Tile Council, Federation House, Station Road, Stoke-on-Trent, ST4 2RU. 0782 45147
	British Floor Covering Manufacturers Association, 125 Queens Road, Brighton BN1 3YW. 0273 33322
Windows	Aluminium Windows Association, 26 Store Street, London WC1E 7EL. 01 637 3578 See also Glass, above.
	There does not appear to be an association of double-glazing manufacturers.
Wood	Forest Products Research Laboratories, Princes Risborough, Aylesbury, Bucks. (ex-directory)
	British Wood Preserving Association, 150 Southampton Row, London WC1. 01 837 8217

General bodies

British Standards Institution, 2 Park Street, London W1A 2BS. 01 629 9000

Building Research Establishment, Carston, Watford, Herts WD2 7JR. 09273 74040

Building Centre, 26 Store Street, London WC1E 7EL. 01 637 8361

Consumers Association, 14 Buckingham Street, London WC2N 6DS. 01 839 1222

Design Council, 28 Haymarket, London SW1Y 4SU. 01 839 8000
HMSO, 51 Nine Elms Lane, London SW8 5DR. 01 211 3000
National House-Building Council, Chiltern Avenue, Amersham, Bucks. HP6 5AP. 02403 4477

Local Government

Where this book refers to 'the town hall' or 'the local authority' it may be difficult to be sure who you should approach. Your local branch library will be able to tell you for certain who is responsible for a particular function in a specific locality, and the *Municipal Year Book* outlines the structure and powers of every authority in the country.

Officers can only give advice, however senior they may be (or may be willing to tell you how they will advise their committee). *Only the authority can give a decision.*

Index